Digital Divide

An Equation Needing a Solution

by

Steven E. Fitch MBA

FIRST EDITION

Designed by Steven E. Fitch MBA

Library of Congress Cataloging-in-Publication Data

Digital Divide: *An Equation Needing a Solution*   .

ISBN: 978-1-4303-0581-1

ACKNOWLEDGMENTS

First and foremost, I wish to thank God for providing me the talent and patience to put pen to paper preparing this book.

I owe more than I can express to the thoughtful and unwavering support of my wife, Cynthia Fitch CPA. Our relationship is a proposition of loving that has lasted a good mark of time and has defied a description on one page, so I won't start here. At this time, I will say thanks – thanks for your patience and putting up with me, and just accepting me with **all** of my flaws.

To my daughter, Jazmine Lanee', thank you for just being you – your love and energy kept my spirits high especially through the tough days. As you grow, always remember, *"keep being you!"*

And finally, I also wish to thank my entire family and friends for the constant encouragement extended to me over the years.

From my first-book experience, I have learned so much. Mainly, no one person writes a book. The understanding, compassion, encouragement and love of others are essential to be successful in anything.

Oh, that my words were written! Oh that they were printed in a book.
~ JOB 19:23

In memory of Seth E. Fitch Jr.

November 29, 1930 – November 1, 2006

Table of Content

INTRODUCTION

"Man cannot discover new oceans, until he has the courage to lose sight of the shore."

I started writing this first as an article while in graduate school, as an external tool for minority students who are considering studying Information Technology (*IT*). Well, the article has come full-circle. This piece of writing was totally different to me. I submitted a complete article on the subject, but towards the end of the assignment, I realized that I had more to share. So with my work and social schedule, I put this document on hold until I could really *re-dedicate* myself. Recently, I had an *epiphany* to buckle down and compile all the information that I wish I had as a student, and well, as it goes, the rest is *my-story*.

About the Author

I began my career more than *sixteen* years ago in the *Information Systems Technology* industry as a database administrator at a Fortune 1000 company. That is where I learned the *ins and outs* of technology and all it had to offer. I was introduced to a number of career paths, such as desktop support (helpdesk), programming, documentation (technical writing) and local area network (LAN) environments, as well as the Internet to name a few.

Fortune 500 list
http://money.cnn.com/magazines/fortune/fortune500/full_list/

In a world of constant changing technology and business strategies, I recognized and understood, early on, that *Information Technology* decisions must be based upon individual needs and goals - especially entities who have limited resources. In order for me to obtain my personal goals, I had to affiliated myself with a select group of successful information systems' professionals who specialize in many different platforms, such as *design and implementation of hardware, software development, internet design and security, technical writing, network operating systems design, and support*, as well as other business industry professionals, such as *accounting, legal, marketing, real estate, retail, etc...* This diverse affiliation currently allows me to create an environment rich with the elements required to successfully meet today's business

---

Digital Divide: An Equation needing a Solution

requirements, while planning for tomorrow's unforeseen advances. In addition, I hope to use my education, experience and expertise to provide a refreshing, yet candid, point of view for individuals and small businesses via my writings and case studies.

At the time of this writing, I have developed and compiled a number of _FREE_ articles surrounding home PC users, small business owners, as well as student's use of technology and various business entities. The _FREE_ articles I have developed are published and distributed quarterly as an e-newsletter, *xChange*™, which has over _hundreds_ of subscribers.

xChange™
http://stevenefitch.com/news.htm

On a personal note, I have my Master's in Business Administration from Keller Graduate School of Management (Chicago – http://keller.edu), a Bachelor's degree in Computer Science from Chicago State University (http://csu.edu) and a number of awards, certifications and other credentials.

To read more about my background, feel free to visit my web site at http://www.stevenefitch.com/bio.htm.

What's special about this book?

You are holding something near and dear to me, and I hope to use this book to start a dialogue to close the gap between the *have's and the have-nots*, as well as inspire people to use technology to further their daily lifestyles. In my writings, I took an easy, straight-line approach while handling the context of this book and jammed it with the most current, useful information possible, as well as included tips for just about everyone who aspires to receive a better understanding of technology. Best yet, your current level of understanding technology doesn't play a major factor in understanding this book. So, don't worry about not having years of technical experience and knowing all of the buzzwords and acronyms. The information you'll find here is very user friendly, easy to read and understandable, plus, firmly grounded into real world analogies.

Now, what you will *not* find in this book is abstract collection of theoretical mumbo-jumbo that sounds good, but doesn't work, isn't practical, or that's clearly not understood. Instead, I've pulled together the best information, strategies and techniques to help aid the process of understanding the ***digital divide***.

This book also provides a thought-provoking pause for use in the march into the *Information Age*. I truly hope to examine the critical role of teacher training, curricular integration and ways to fund a long-term solution to the equation of the ***digital divide***.

Ultimately, I want this book to be fun – it reflects on my personal belief that learning doesn't have to be boring. It is imperative that people learn and take full advantage of the importance of technology.

You cannot teach a man anything; you can only help him find it within himself. ~ Galileo

Special icons

I've added icons throughout this book to illustration certain facts, concepts, and tips that emphasizes important points about technology. You'll find the following icons in the margin of a given paragraph:

New terminology (*glossary*)

Case study

Sometimes you need advice from a professional. So what I've done is listed organizations (*companies or individuals*) that I'm affiliated with that can give you additional assistance in the area.

Very important piece of advice, tip or shortcut.

Basic questions about a particular subject or topic.

Recommended Web site to visit.

Index number

(or footnote)

Further recommended reading on a particular subject.

Glossary of new terminology

Like every other profession, *Information Technology* has **A LOT** of acronyms and jargon that make no sense, except to people familiar with computers. For starters, a computer is commonly called *PC*, or *personal computer*. Whew! For your convenience, I have supplied you with a list of new terms and definitions to help assist you as you read through the book.

Glossary

Access to additional information

www.stevenefitch.com

If you visit *www.stevenefitch.com* and click the books' title: *Digital Divide: An Equation Needing a Solution*, then navigate to *Book Extras / Missing CD-ROM*. There you will find a neat, organized list of extra items to further develop and improve your experience with this text, such as, section-by-section list of freeware, shareware, lots of offline information, resources, case studies, etc… mentioned in this book. As noted on the back cover, having the software online instead of including a CD-ROM saved you $5 on the production cost of this book.

The web site also offers updates and any corrections. To see the updates, follow the same procedures listed above, but instead navigate to *Updates*. In fact, you're invited and encouraged to submit updates, corrections, as well as conversation pieces in my *Blog* area.

Blog

If you would like a CD-ROM, I can ship one to you at an additional cost.

NOTE: *I use business card size CD-ROMs, which contain all of the above information plus additional FREEWARE applications and utilities.* You can contact me electronically at my web site or email. I'm also available via snail mail at the following:

Steven E. Fitch MBA
4710 Lincoln Hwy, Suite 350
Matteson, IL 60443
www.stevenefitch.com/digitaldivide
digitaldivide@sefitch.com

If you study to remember, you will forget,

but if you study to understand, you will remember. ~ Anonymous

Chapter 1: What is Digital Divide?

The future has already arrived. It's just not evenly distributed yet. ~ William Gibson

Digital divide has a wide-range of definitions and concepts surrounding it. According to [i]Wikipedia™, FREE online encyclopedia, defines it as a social / political issue referring to the socio-economic gap between communities that have access to computers and the Internet and those who do not. In other markets, it refers to gaps that exist between groups regarding their ability to use technology effectively, due to differing levels of literacy and technical skills, as well as the gap between those groups that have access to quality, useful digital content and those that do not.

http://wikipedia.com

The term, *digital divide*, became very popular among concerned parties, such as scholars, equal-rights organizations, policy makers and advocacy groups, in the late 1990s.
In the early days of *digital divide* analysis, the availability of Internet access at an affordable cost was the key issue. Social penetrations of the Internet and technological advances have rendered this distinction as the chief concern of the *digital divide* obsolete. Many people can get free access in local Internet Cafes, work, schools, libraries, etc... Broadly speaking, the difference is not necessarily determined by the access to the Internet alone. It can also refer to lifestyles and social environment – *have's versus the have-nots*. Today, the argument has moved on to skills, resources and literacy, as well as the training of people *versus* lifestyle.
In my research, I have found that the number of Americans connected to the world's information infrastructure is soaring. Nevertheless, *digital divide* still exists, and, in many cases, is actually widening. Monitories, low-income persons, the less educated and children of single-parent households, particularly when they reside in rural areas, are among the groups that lack access to information resources.

The following gaps with regard to home Internet access are representative of:

- *the gaps between White and Hispanic households, and between White and Black households, are now approximately five percentage points larger than they were in 2003.*
- *the **digital divide**, based on education and income levels, have also increased in the last year alone. Between 2004 and 2005, the divide between those at the highest and lowest education levels increased 25 percent, and the divide between those at the highest and lowest income levels grew 29 percent.*

As previously stated, the good news is that Americans are more connected than ever before. Thus, access to computers and the Internet has soared for people in all demographic groups and geographic locations. At the end of 2005, over 40 percent of American households owned computers, and a little more than one-quarter of all households had Internet access.

Accompanying this good news, however, is the persistence of the ***digital divide*** between the information rich (*such as Whites, Asians/Pacific Islanders, those with higher incomes, those more educated, and dual-parent households*) and the information poor (*such as those who are younger, those with lower incomes and education levels, certain minorities, and those in rural areas or central cities*). The 2005 data reveal significant disparities, including the following:

- *urban households with incomes of $75,000 and higher are more than twenty times more likely to have access to the Internet than rural households at the lowest income levels, and more than nine times as likely to have a computer at home.*
- *whites are more likely to have access to the Internet from home than Blacks or Hispanics.*
- *Black and Hispanic households are approximately one-third as likely to have home Internet access as households of Asian/Pacific Islander descent, and roughly two-fifths as likely as White households.*
- *regardless of race & income level, Americans living in rural areas are lagging behind in Internet access. Indeed, at the lowest income levels, those in urban areas are more than twice as likely to have Internet access as those earning the same income in rural areas.*

Nevertheless, as you can see, the news is not all bleak. For those Americans with incomes of $75,000 and higher, the divide between Whites and Blacks has actually narrowed considerably in the last year. This finding suggests that the most affluent American families, irrespective of race, are connecting to the Internet.

Technology is a single life's component, which influences people's ability to acquire what they want in their personal, interpersonal, career endeavors, financial position, environmental and spiritual lives.

Digital Divide: An Equation needing a Solution

Some skeptics point out that not every gap is a problem. [ii]Michael Powell, former chairman of the Federal Communication Commission (FCC), stated that there's a Mercedes divide and he'd like to have one but couldn't afford one.

And he followed up defining his position by stating *"the minute a new and innovative technology is introduced in the market, there is a divide unless it is equitably distributed among every part of society, and that is just an unreal understanding of an American capitalistic system. I'm not meaning to be completely flip about this-- I think it's an important social issue-- but it shouldn't be used to justify the notion of, essentially, the socialization of deployment of the infrastructure[iii]."*

In his sarcastic analogy, Mr. Powell was stating that a person making a choice to purchase a car has a choice – go high-end with a Mercedes-Benz™, or go to middle of the road and select a Buick™ - get what you can afford. In any case, Mercedes-Benz™' vehicles doesn't stop one from traveling from one place to another. So, those that can't afford a Mercedes-Benz™' don't have the same choices presented to them. To his point, I would argue the Internet is a universal service providing links to tons of information, and it is available to *everyone* who can connect, while Mercedes-Benz™ is an individual product line to those who can afford it. So along the lines of technology, is it okay for people who can afford to purchase technological advances to have them while those who cannot shouldn't?

Let's make no mistake about it, the notion that some people have access to information than others, is not new. [iv]The knowledge gap hypothesis, in communications studies, first formulated by Tichendor, Donohue, & Olien (1970), suggests that there is a chronic gap of knowledge that different sectors of society possess. The subsequent research seems to suggest that the gap is smaller in the arena of knowledge about local issues and matters personally relevant to the recipients. The gap was also thought to reduce as television replaces newspaper as a source of knowledge. Compared to newspapers, television requires less literacy, and it is considered a more passive medium. It was thought that the advent of the Internet might reverse this change, since it is predominantly a text medium. It is also the case that users of the Internet may need more skills to navigate through vast amount of information rather than passively receiving information feed from newspaper or television as well as search for information a person desires instantly.

Imagine for a moment. . . [v]June 19th 1865, which commemorates the day when slaves in Texas first learned that President Abraham Lincoln signed the Emancipation Proclamation, granting them their freedom after hundred of years of servitude. Well, President Lincoln signed the proclamation in 1863, nearly two and half years earlier than the news reached the people. Sure, many scholars argue that the way information spread in those days was slow, thus, the people who had the news could with hold it – keeping it from the freed slaves. The point I'm making is it took two and half years for people to obtain such vital information regardless of people withholding it. Now imagine if this occurred today. . . businesses would crumble. . . food industry would collapse. . . health industry would come to a complete halt. . . Just think how you feel when your cable television is out, or your cellular phone provider is down, or even better yet, the lights in your house are out. Imagine how horrible life would be without advancements in storm early warnings (i.e., tornado's, hurricanes, blizzard, etc…). Today, we have access to more information, via television, radio, and/or Internet, than ever before. In fact, there's so much information available that people have to pick-and-choose what they have an interest in.

A common, underlying philosophy practiced in today's society is based on the belief that an individual's life is compromised of many interdependent parts that function in harmony with each other, rather than in isolation, is absolutely more valid today than ever.

More later on the Internet and its power of information access.

Digital Divide: An Equation needing a Solution

Is the digital divide hype & propaganda?

The divide between those with access to technologies and those without is one of America's leading economic and civil rights issues. One could argue, for thousands of years, there have always been the *"haves"* and *"have-nots."* In fact, even in the Bible there were *haves* and *have-nots.*

For example, Job, Abraham, Joseph, David, and Solomon were all rich men, while there were many surrounding kingdoms that did without. But in this case, these men demonstrated that the purpose of working is not to obtain wealth for our own gratification, but to help those less fortunate *(Eph. 4:28).*

http://bible.com

The Bible also contains over *one thousand* references to wealth and property. That's twice as many references to faith and prayer. I don't mean to offend anyone, but to illustrate that this division has existed from the beginning of time.

In some respects it does seem like a good idea to have separate categories such as the *"haves"* and *"have-nots."* On the surface it allows for people to aspire to achieve more and continue to work hard towards a goal. But unfortunately, in most cases, the people who are working the hardest, don't always get ahead at that same rate nor have the same resources or opportunities - *divide.* In fact, statistics show that people that work more than 40 hours a week tend to make less progress in their career endeavors than people who are established in the workforce.

I would definitely say that dealing with the ***digital divide*** isn't hype or propaganda. There may be some that use this situation for political or social gain, but the fact of the matter is the ***digital divide*** really demonstrates a lot of obstacles that are somewhat inherit in our lives. Facing the issue is one thing, but soundly resolving the situation is much more important.

Questions to ask yourself?

How often do you use a computer (outside of work)?

1. *Never*
2. *1-5 hours per week*
3. *6-12 hours per week*
4. *13-18 hours per week*
5. *19+ hours per week*

 Excluding work, where do you use a PC the most?

1. *Home*
2. *School*
3. *Library*
4. *Work*
5. *other...*

Many people have the option of accessing the Internet from more than one place. A person can connect from home, a school, library, or community center, or a combination of these locations. As of 2004, 44.8% of *all* Americans access the Internet at home, 57% use it at some location other than their home, while approximately two-thirds do not use it all (outside of work).

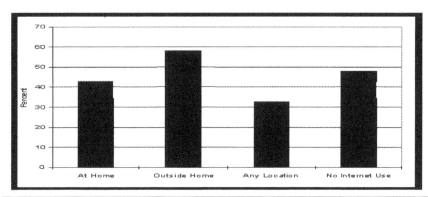

	At Home	Outside Home	Any Location	No Internet Use
U.S. Persons	44.8	58.0	32.7	42.1

Digital Divide: An Equation needing a Solution

Based on the above statistics, most people only have access, or should I say fast access, in location other than home, such as library, school, work (or private office location), cafés, etc. On average, people with computers at home spend over fifteen hours a week using them (outside of work), and those who have the Internet at home, spend, on average, nine hours of that time on the Web.

While the Internet is widely seen as a young person's medium, it is striking that users of all ages spend, on average, roughly the same amount of time accessing it. The heaviest users, interestingly, are not the youngest adults, but people thirty to thirty-nine. On average, they spend twenty-one hours a week on computers, including nine hours on the Internet, excluding the use of e-mail.

Another surprise is that, while more educated people are more likely than less educated people to be users of the Internet, the amount of time spent using it does not vary much (only between six and seven hours a week) between high school graduates, college graduates or people with post graduate degrees. This may be particular true with those with families.

Contradictory speaking, many people do not have access for numerous reasons. Multiple reasons exist as to why households with computers at home have never used the Internet there. In the 2003 [vi]Chicago Public School supplement survey, the most common response given was that the household's occupants "*don't want*" such access (25.7%). The second major reason among respondents concerns "*cost*" (16.8%), which is further disaggregated into the monthly service charge (9.7%), the need to make a toll call in order to reach one's ISP (4.8%), and other costs (2.3%). Following cost are such categories as "*can use elsewhere*" (9.6%), "*no time*" (8.7%), computer not capable"(8.3%), "*future access planned*" (but none at home currently) (7.5%), "*concern with children*" (6.0%), and "*not useful*" (5.6%). Some people gave "*not user friendly*" (2.7%) and "*problem with service provider in home area*" (1.3 %) as reasons for not having Internet access at home. Myriad other responses whose percentages are quite small appear under the headings "*other cost*" and "*other*".

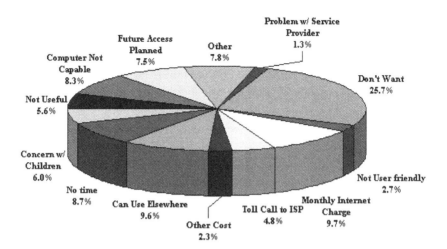

I have found that the failure of African Americans to use the Internet is not only due to income, it is also a problem of education. At the time of this writing, the [vii]Department of Commerce has released its *sixth* annual report on the use of the Internet. A major conclusion of that report, published throughout the nation, is that minorities are still lagging behind whites (or other races) in their use of the Internet.

http://commerce.gov/

There are many proactive measures that can be used for computers today. For starters, through networked computers, students can obtain and share information in the classroom more efficiently, as well as collaborate with their circle of peers from all around the world almost instantly. Additionally, students can get information online, which may otherwise be unachievable without spending lots of time at the library or study hall. However, without this access, they are denied these educational opportunities and are entirely disconnected from the powers of the technology that will be essential for earning a decent living. As much as this new technology can equalize opportunities for students of all backgrounds, the absence of these basic resources – computers, software, instruction, and Internet Service Providers (*ISP*) – has the potential of widening gaps

---

Digital Divide: An Equation needing a Solution

between populations. I will expand more on this topic in *Chapter 4: Education Divide* section.

Furthermore, within diverse communities, people with low incomes and less education are among the groups often is lacking access to information resources. It may be safe to assume when you put technology on a priority list of life's necessities, well, it (technology) falls lower and lower on the list.

Example:

- *Housing*
- *Utilities (heat, light, telephone, cable)*
- *Food*
- *Education*
- *Clothes and personal items*
- *Transportation*
- *Entertainment*
- *and then technology*

This **digital divide** cuts through society on all levels: *racial, economic, educational and even gender lines.* In addition, girls are often not presented the same opportunities and encouragement to develop computer skills as boys. Many assume girls may *not* feel comfortable with computers. They may be elbowed out at the computer by boys or not necessarily supported, do not have role models in the industry – especially girls of color. There are a lot of assumptions here that need to be addressed and resolved, but in short, everyone – girls and boys of all races need to have access to the same information, at any given time, at any location - evenly. See the *Chapter 2: Gender Divide* for further discuss.

In summary, the most important reasons why certain households have never used the Internet is not that they "*don't want it,*" people still feel computers are still too expensive and do not truly understand their importance. Although the former is the more common cop-out used, the cost factor continues to dominates among low-income groups, Hispanics, single-parent families, and the unemployed. Policymakers should, therefore, consider the role of cost as a deterrent to expanding online access and resources.

What's to gain by resolving the digital divide equation?

In the fore mentioned conclusion are assumptions that should be considered. This lag is an historical commonplace for minority groups. There is a major assumption in the minority community that in order to engage computers and technology, one has to be technically trained. Hence, many shy away from using electronic technologies because they are not technically trained. That is a poorly reasoned decision. Today, it is very difficult for anyone, affluent and/or educated, or blue collar, to compete unless they are computer literate. Indeed, one can't begin to understand the fullness of their importance until one begins using computers and the Internet. Most scholars acknowledge that the Internet is a tool that we should master for numerous reasons.

The Department of Commerce's report states that households with incomes of above $75,000 were more than five times more likely to have access to the Net than those with incomes of $10,000 or less. And of households of $15,000 – 35,000, one-third

of the whites had PC's, and 19% of Blacks and Latinos had them. But this is not only a problem of income; it is also a problem of education. [viii]Dr. Jackson, in his

---

Digital Divide: An Equation needing a Solution

essay on Black Violence, depicts a situation where the oppress turn on themselves out of a sense of confusion and frustration because of oppression. However, we cannot excuse ourselves when we do not use available tools that can aid in our own

Economic or educational development. We have the capacity, but we must see the need. Because of our lack of use of the Internet and other electronic media, minorities become prey to these media-savvy entities. Thus, our communities are manipulated by plastering seemingly friendly faces that step intensely to their script, as they court our readership, and, in fact, offer nothing but a similar face that does not represent your best interest. It is tragic that minorities have not seen the significance of electronic media and technological advances, other than TV, and that media's impact on their lives and economics concerning mass media has such a profound power in our community, where perception is *ninety-nine* percent visual *versus* factual. In addition, we are known to spend more money on tangible items *versus* education. More on this subject in the coming section – *Bling versus Bytes*. Indeed, this is a hot topic and covered extensively at the National Association for the Advancement of Colored People® (NAACP®) annual convention.

http://naacp.org

So, you ask why is technology important? If the previous paragraphs didn't answer this question, **keep reading**. There are many ways businesses take advantage of technology these days. From small, ma-and-pa businesses to mega, Fortune 1000 companies new products, and with the continuing plummeting costs of technology have positioned companies today to be more competitive in their respective market places with a minimum investment.

For instance, ma-and-pa stores can analyze their inventory and learn what sells and what doesn't, in what quantities, to whom, what season, at what margin, and just about anything else we might want to know just like Fortune 1000 companies. This sounds like a story about Wal-Mart™, but the truth is, technology has made the same platforms used by mega companies affordable to small businesses. The difference, of course, is the ability to attract employees that help companies achieve these objectives. Smaller businesses do not have the same capital resources to achieve this type of infrastructure alone. In most cases, reasoning like this is cliché and equivalent to "*Casting the baby out with the bath water.*" But, I've learned or should I say adopted "*Save the baby, but not the bath water.*" I believe that is reasonable and fair. This same reasoning may be a factor in the hesitancy of African Americans and other minorities to use the Internet, even for their own help, but such primitive reasoning should be put away. The time is now to accept and learn how to use these resources to enhance your lifestyle and gain a competitive edge.

Digital Divide: An Equation needing a Solution

Name one occupation that doesn't require a computer to operate?

Salons / Barber / Spa	use a date book to keep appointments
Dentist / Doctor	use for date book, accounts payable, accounts receivable as well as patient information
Lawyer	research and document preparation
Accountant / Tax	preparation of taxes with correct calculations and future retrieval as needed
Writer / Journalism / Minister	typing and saving documents, articles, books, etc...
Teachers	lesson plans, grades (calculations)
Custodian Engineer	logging time, measuring disposal and inventory
Construction / Architecture	access to database of construction codes in a given city / state, ability to visual see the construction site even before it is built, as well as save drawings for future use
Photographer	ability to save photos for an infinite length of time and provide customers the ability to view them electronically before printing and/or purchasing items not wanted (cost effective)
Politician	access statistics of the current population, voting swings, trends, etc...
Secretary	access to real-time date book and contact listings, document retrieval
Retail	access to inventory, selling points, profit margins, etc...
Transportation *(trucker driver, train conductor, pilot, etc)*	provide these employees with accurate and up-to-date information pertaining to travel conditions for safety reasons and convenience

to name a few. . . Were you able to name one? If so, send me an email at digitaldivide@sefitch.com.

More than likely, you were unable to name one. Now do you see how important technology is today? Now imagine how important technology will be tomorrow?

Case Study – Technology within the Church

With the advancement of technology, churches are finding themselves in an interesting predicament, which turns the church into *two* churches: *traditional and contemporary*. The *traditional* church is more about being present in the sanctuary, taking hand-written notes, attending church meetings, bible school, singing in harmony with the choir, and going physically out into society as a group to provide assistance and guidance. This demographic has been around since the beginning of time and just work without a hiccup. In fact, it's the only way many people over the age of forty-five know how to attend church. Thus, the people who make up this demographic are usually without personal access to technology (or very limited access).

While the *contemporary* services (*or kindly termed Gen-Xers*) are more intangible, it provides people of this demographic a very viable resource to praise God - *technology*. People of this group, can attend church from anywhere in the world, live or previously recorded, via the use of their computer and the Internet.

I've found that in most cases, church services are already hi-tech with complex audio / video equipment that almost emulates a rock and roll concert, or a Hollywood television set which blurs the lines between entertainment and reverence; consumption and worship; spirituality and distraction, but I digress.

These types of advancements in the church are very useful for people that travel and/or find themselves home and unable to attend regular service. Furthermore, this group is constantly looking for ways to use technology to introduce people *globally* to Jesus Christ, where church services can be heard and even viewed on television or over the Internet, as well as collect donations via an *e-Commerce* solution.

Digital Divide: An Equation needing a Solution

Technology today has provided churches with a number of advancements, such as

- *the ability to management the business side of services more efficiently with the use of accounting and database software*
- *the use of the Internet to market the Church and its beliefs*
- *the ability for members to monitor tithing (or yearly pledges), attendance, events, etc...*
- *the use of a projector can be used to show the words to a hymn for all to sing along with instead of, or in addition to hymn books*
- *providing members, as well as visitors access to fundraisers and items available for purchase – e-Commerce (i.e., tapes, CD, DVD's, sermons, books, calendars, etc...)*
- *the use of presentation software which can be used to teach Sunday school lessons, help with traditional note taking, while word processors can be used to archive sermons and take (record) notes*
- *digital audio equipment to provide church members the ability to purchase the sermon and/or songs heard while at church services*
- *the use of digital camera as well as video to take and record services and events*
  . . . to name a few

In a poll, at a church, a congregation was asked to stand up. They were then asked those who have access to a DVD player or VCR to remain standing - and the rest to sit down. To their surprise they had a good portion of our members sit down –mostly consisting of elderly people. Then this same congregation was asked who had access to a PC at home? A few people sat down – mainly people over *fifty*. In another related poll, people who attend church services for the first time were asked how they found the church. Interesting enough - many answered word of mouth from other members. . . others stated that they first looked to see if the church had a website, and more importantly - if their website will let them know about programs offered for their children, themselves, the community and *streams*? Online tithing?

Streaming

To assist this demographic in the church, there are a lot companies providing the means for church's to take advantage of technology.

http://streamingfaith.com
http://E-Zekiel.com
http://webempoweredchurch.com

Streamingfaith.com*: world's largest faith-based video portal.*

E-Zekiel.com: *providing Christian organizations with easy-to-use communication tools.*

Web Empowered Church - (WEC): *designed to help churches around the world apply Internet technology.*

In short, churches are being forced to make many decisions that they have never been faced with before, such as to provide their parishioners with the ability to use the World Wide Web to extend their church community, communication tools (e-mail), provide blogging tools, online chats, forums, as well as prayer listings.

One thing to keep in mind, especially in this case study, as well as making a decision on the use of technology in a church; technology *does **not*** make the church. It can, however, enhance the church community and allow your teachings to reach an audience never before witnessed – 24 hours a day / 7 days a week.

NOTE: All trademarks mentioned are the property of their respective owners. I am not recommending one product, service or web site over another.

Chapter 2: Racial and Gender Divide

My challenge to the young people is to pick up where this generation has left off; to

create a world where every man, woman and child is not limited,

except by their own capabilities. ~ Colin Powell

I have found that the failure of minorities to use the Internet is not only a problem of income; it is also a problem of race and gender. According to [ix]Larry Irving, former Assistant Secretary of Commerce, America's **digital divide** is fast becoming a *"racial ravine,"* and this comes from one of America's leading economic and civil rights leaders. The numbers tell a shocking story and it all begins with access. *Eighty-four* percent of schools where minority enrollment is less than *six* percent have access to the Internet and computer classes, compared to *sixty-three* percent of schools where minority access is more than *fifty* percent. Furthermore, whites are more than twice as likely to have access to the Internet from home as African-Americans or Hispanics have from any location. Without basic access, there can be no discussion of skill-building, instructional quality and appropriate use of technology.

Thus, the **digital divide** has turned into a *"racial ravine"* when one looks at access among households of different races and ethnic origins. With regard to computers, the gap between White and Black households *grew 39.2%* (from a 16.8 percentage point difference to a 23.4 percentage point difference) between 2000 and 2005. For White versus Hispanic households, the gap similarly *rose by 42.6%* (from a 14.8 point gap to 21.1 point gap).

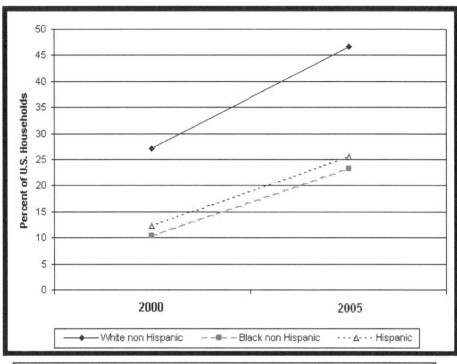

	White non Hispanic	Black non Hispanic	Hispanic
2000	27.1	10.3	12.3
2005	46.6	23.2	25.5
14.8 vs. 21.1 percentage point difference between Whites and Hispanics			
16.8 vs. 23.4 percentage point difference between Whites and Blacks			

These sample surveys aren't very precise, but however, you can obtain a visual of the margin between ethnic groups. And based on this, it seems that a significantly smaller percentage of American blacks use the Worldwide Web than their white fellow citizens.

Why?   While everyone from cosmic conspiracy paranoids to lonely-hearts clubbers visit and use the Internet. So, why do so few minorities participate? Is it something intrinsic in the medium? Or dare I ask, is the Internet somehow racist? Is the issue purely economics?

Let me attempt to answer these questions with a story: *A colleague of mine, while in college at a prominent white campus, once had an Asian neighbor, who thought he was hip and cool. The Asian neighbor knew all of the latest slang and songs, and wanted to be recognized as an open-minded person especially among the blacks. Well, with this, he was also a pothead and ever so often he would sit out and smoke a joint. On several occasions people would ask my colleague does he smoke? He would reply 'No.' this went on for a couple of weeks and finally he grew tired of this line of questioning from other neighbors. So he approached the Asian neighbor and asked him to stop smoking pot on the property. His Asian neighbor said "I thought Black people were cool."*

The above story is a testament to the ignorance of the Black culture. Yes, Black folks brought you jazz. Yes, we are famed in the popular mindset for adapting forms of music, speech and worship to suit our own needs. We have also historically been stereotyped for congenital lawlessness. Yet, in fact, we are the product of a culture that is among the most conventional, and yes, even timid in modern America.

Additionally, only 35 years from legalized segregation and enforced second-class citizenship, Black Americans still honor the idea of a firm foothold in the middle class with all of the virtues (and vices) that it implies. We are the farthest people from cool in this case.

The Internet, however, is cool. The Internet is the direct opposite of traditional middle-class virtues. New, chaotic, shamelessly undisciplined, alternately revolutionary and reactionary, the Internet, by nature, butts heads with entrenched African-American cultural truths. It mocks some of our fundamental beliefs, our core desires.

[x]Malcolm Casselle, co-founder of NetNoir (www.netnoir.com), stated "African-Americans just don't perceive the value of the Internet." That's because the Internet can't help us achieve our '50s and '60s ideals. We still want the corporate American dream -- a good steady job with benefits, a shot at the executive suite -- while the rest of the country moves on to dreams of entrepreneurship and self-employment. Thus, suggesting a change with African-American traditions is often greeted with dismay or dismissal. Not only are we outrageously conservative in our cultural outlook, we can be awfully self-righteous about it as well.

Collectively, we fail to realize, however, that by the time we get the results we seek, they will be what no one else wants, and we will have foregone opportunities like those

Digital Divide: An Equation needing a Solution

offered by the Internet and other high-tech, chaos-theory-driven engines onto which the majority will have climbed and ridden away.

In my humble opinion, I suggested that Black Americans should look beyond marching in the streets to gain political power. We are American traditionalists in the extreme. I must admit, I am torn between being proud of that fact and being irked by it. On the one hand, it was that traditionalism -- our middle-class strivings and solidly Christian social morals that kept us from violence, while this country's majority made sport of abusing us. After all, the Christian right does not hold street rallies, yet has gained political muscle. The Internet is among the tools the right uses to solidify and mobilize its power base. I suggest and recommend that Black Americans should do the same.

Another tradition, to which we keep, whether out of pride, or fear (or both), is one of place. The Internet is considered a place. We call it cyber*space.* We *visit* a Web site. The Internet is presented as a series of landscapes or neighborhoods.

The Internet isn't tangible nor can it be completed like an amusement park. In addition, it cannot be segregated. Now any group or demographic can have favorite sites, chat rooms, forums, etc. but walk into any integrated college dining hall and you will find a majority of the people of the same race sitting together. There is safety in numbers, and American Blacks have a long history that makes us crave that safety.

Through decades and generations of cross burnings, redlining, beatings, bombings and harassment, American Blacks are wary of mixed environments and the Internet is no exception.

Some suggest that the Internet is the great color barrier dissolver because in cyberspace, one doesn't know what race or religion one's audience or conversation partner might be. But that's only true in a very narrow sense. A Black American can do business on the Web without facing what even ideologically pure Black conservative [xi]Rep. Gary Franks, R-Conn., called the majority's distaste for "the idea of putting money in a Black man's pocket." But suggesting that American Blacks would take comfort in conversing with those who would not show hatred or bigotry or cultural chauvinism toward them only because the other party didn't know they were Black -- that's insulting in the extreme. Such a suggestion could only come from a mindlessly, liberally chauvinistic mind, like that of the college Asian neighbor who thought all Black folks were open to marijuana.

Let me make one point perfectly clear: *cyber place is no haven*. The hatreds, that are part of this nation's very soul, live there too. Plus *new* types of criminals – [xii]cyber-criminals and they can be categorized as follows:

- **Financial** - *crimes that disrupt businesses' ability to conduct 'e-commerce' (or electronic commerce).*
- **Piracy** - *the act of copying copyrighted material. The personal computer and the Internet both offer new mediums for committing an 'old' crime. Online theft is defined as any type of 'piracy' that involves the use of the Internet to market or distribute creative works protected by copyright.*
- **Hacking** - *the act of gaining unauthorized access to a computer system or network and in some cases making unauthorized use of this access. Hacking is also the act by which other forms of cyber-crime (e.g., fraud, terrorism, etc.) are committed.*
- **Cyber-terrorism** - *the effect of acts of hacking designed to cause terror. Like conventional terrorism, `e-terrorism' is classified as such if the result of hacking is to cause violence against persons or property, or at least cause enough harm to generate fear.*
- **Online Pornography** - *according to 18 USC 2252 and 18 USC 2252A, possessing or distributing child pornography is against federal law and under 47 USC 223 distributing pornography of any form to a minor is illegal. The Internet is merely a new medium for this `old' crime, but how best to regulate this global medium of communication across international boundaries and age groups has sparked a great deal of controversy and debate.*
- **In Schools** - w*hile the Internet can be a unique educational and recreational resource for children, it is important that they are educated about how to safely and responsibly use this powerful tool. The founding goal of this project is to encourage empowering children through knowledge of the law, their rights, and how best to prevent misuse of the Internet.*

Digital Divide: An Equation needing a Solution

Since the Internet is a place, instead of an institution, it holds particular promise. No one's sense of white self and white worth is invested in it. It can truly be, and be seen as, ours as much as anyone else's. There are precious few nationwide places of culture and commerce in which that can be said.

The Internet could be an extraordinary disseminator of true African-American culture, not the sociopolitical antics that the majority, and too many of us accept as that culture, an extraordinary political tool and a boon to Black business people. But only if we are finally willing to forego the dreams of *terra firma*, to which we've hitched our star for all of our postwar history. We must acknowledge that the world into which we so desperately sought entree is dying -- and we, like the majority, must embrace new and untested worlds if we are to prosper.

terra firma

Rather than avoid the place, or retreating to safe ground, find familiar territory -- we should slough off our conventionalities and hack some new trails through this principally white territory. We've got to embrace some anarchy for once in our history.

Disparity between gender gaps

Even when race, income and educational levels are set aside, there is a ***digital divide*** between men and women. According to Wikipedia, a [xiii]**gender gap** generally refers to the systemic differences in the social and economic position of men and women, or boys and girls. There is a debate to what extent this is the result of gender differences or because of discrimination. The widespread mechanization of industry has been accompanied by a shift in gender differentials in highly industrialized countries. However, this closing of the gender gap has not necessarily been followed in less industrialized countries.

Although women use the Internet in greater numbers than men[xiv], the number of women who are information technology professionals—producers of information technology rather than simply consumers—lags far behind that of men. Women still comprise less than a quarter of information technology professionals, only *eight* percent of information technology engineers, and no more than *five* percent of information technology management. The percentage of women earning degrees in computer science has declined steadily since 1998 and the attrition rate among women computer science students is higher than among men. In particular, minority women make up not more than *two* percent of information technology professionals in the United States. Furthermore, research has indicated that these percentages will decline.

The gender disparity in interest to learn about information technology is already firmly entrenched at the undergraduate level. According to the Department of Commerce, only *1.1* percent of undergraduate women select information technology disciplines as compared to *3.3* percent of male undergraduates in 2000, and the percentage of women earning bachelor's degrees in information technology fields has dropped steadily since 1998. In the words of the U.S. Office of Technology Policy:

Women—who comprise *51* percent of the population and earn more than *half* of all bachelor-level degrees awarded—earn about *one-quarter* of the bachelor-level computer and information sciences degrees awarded by U.S. academic institutions. More disturbing is the trend line: the share of all computer science degrees awarded to women in the United States has fallen steadily from a peak of *35.8* percent in 2000, to only *27.5* percent in 1998—the lowest level since 1989.

These statistics, on the college level, imply that by the time women select majors in college, they may have already decided against information technology professions. The existence of this gender gap, which might be termed the "*gendered digital production divide*," has been acknowledged repeatedly in Congress[xiv] and internationally. Despite repeated acknowledgement, only limited legislative and private sector efforts to eliminate this gender gap in information technology production have been implemented. Meanwhile, the social importance of information technology was fundamentally altered between late 1998 and 2001. No substantive legislative attention has been paid to the gendered production divide in this post Internet boom era, and arguably the last two decades of efforts has been misdirected and ineffective in the aggregate. The limited legislative efforts to date to increase numbers of women among information technology professionals may have failed partially because they have been primarily focused on adults. Gender disparities in information technology career interest are traceable throughout the educational system. In 2001, girls comprised only *nine* percent of high school students taking information technology related advanced placement (AP) exams.

Digital Divide: An Equation needing a Solution

Therefore, girls' self-selection away from computers occurs before the college level. Consequently, a more promising point for intervention is during girls' early high school and junior high school years.

Additionally speaking, according to the New York Times, women earn only *18* percent of the doctorates awarded in computer science in the United States, and only *12* percent of all engineering PhD's. While making up nearly *half* of the nation's workforce, women account for just *22* percent of the employed scientists and engineers. This division between women and men begins in school between girls and boys. According to many studies, girls still do not receive the same attention as boys in technology, mat and science classes, and they are not encouraged to pursue technology as a career field. Teen social dynamics also discourage girls from pursuing interests in technology-related fields. Until men and women are treating equally, these disparaging numbers will continue to grow at a much faster rate since women out-number men.

Why Blacks don't use, like, or trust technology

As previously stated, American Blacks have a disproportionate fear relative to the Internet. In short, we have traditionally been distrustful of people asking for information. Many have privacy concerns that go back to a number of issues in the community, as well as society.

At the time of this writing, data shows that Americans are very concerned about invasions of their privacy caused by accessing the Internet. Almost *two-thirds* of America's are either "*very concerned*" or "*somewhat concerned*" about confidentiality on the Internet. There are legitimate concerns regarding the collection and transmission of personal information via the Internet, especially information gathered from children. The Administration has set forth an [xv]Electronic Bill of Rights, proposing that every consumer have: *the right to choose whether her personal information is disclosed; the right to know how, when and how much of that information is being used; the right to see that information; and the right to know if information is accurate and to be able to correct it if it is not.*

The Administration believes that the private sector should take the lead in implementing meaningful, consumer-friendly privacy regimes. I would like for companies to take additional steps to notify customers of their privacy policies, process consumer privacy preferences, protect customer data, and handle inquiries and complaints. Several promising private sector initiatives are underway, such as BBBOnline® and TRUSTe®, which require merchants to adhere to fair trade practices. These programs provide a seal of appeal to businesses that post privacy policies that meet certain criteria.

www.truste.org

www.bbbonline.org

Parents are also concerned about their children's safety while using the Internet. The same data shows that one of the reasons that households with a computer have never used the Internet is "*concerns with children.*" The Administration is committed to empowering parents, teachers, and other guardians with tools to keep children safe while online.

The Administration has encouraged private sector initiatives, such as "*One Click Away,*" which are designed to give parents technology and educational resources to protect their children from material that they deem to be inappropriate and to know who to contact when their children encounter dangerous situations online. The Administration has also promoted the concept of "*green spaces*" -- educational, age-appropriate, noncommercial content that is easily identifiable for families online.

www.getnetwise.org

Digital Divide: An Equation needing a Solution

Race-based Business Decisions

A good example of tough decisions made by minority business people, interested in pursuing technical opportunities would be *E. David Ellington*. More than ten years ago, when E. David Ellington decided to start [xvi]**NetNoir, Inc.** (www.netnoir.com), a leading multimedia company promoting, creating and distributing distinctive Black/African American programming and commercial applications for all forms of interactive media in the San Francisco Bay area. During his start-up, he was faced with a difficult choice: locate his offices in heavily Black Oakland, instead of with all the other Web start-ups in San Francisco's mostly white South Park area, known as Multimedia Gulch?

http://www.netnoir.com

Ellington deciding that his first allegiance was to Blacks online, and that he could best serve that community if he first built a presence in the heart of the high-tech industry, so he chose South Park.

He was developing a tech-driven media company; therefore he needed to be around people doing cutting-edge technology. I'm certain he thought long and hard whether to stay in Oakland in his majority black community - even when that might have limited his potential growth, strategic partnerships, and ability to leverage deals.

NetNoir's dilemma reflects the thorny complexity of race in cyberspace. The online world was just beginning to acknowledge the deep well of feelings and history that underlie the American Blacks' experience; the vague utopian heritage of the Internet has led much of the online industry to act as though race simply disappears as an issue once we shed the physical world for the virtual. Oakland or San Francisco? That's not supposed to matter in the new world of the information super highway. Right? But of course it does.

The bottom line is minorities still make up a disproportionately small percentage of the American online population. Ellington estimated that, out of America Online's 40 million-plus subscribers (at the time), at least *35%* are Black and he expects that number to continue to grow.

A similar dilemma has long faced the leaders of the U.S. newspaper industry, whose newsroom rosters have often failed to reflect the changing urban population. In one view of the problem, publishers will find Black readers or users only if they can better integrate their staffs and the content of their publications.

In a similar disparity, print publications have long been under pressure to increase minority employment and have only made limited progress. Despite efforts over the past 20 years by unions and the American Society of Newspaper Editors, minorities -- including Blacks, Hispanics and Asian Americans -- comprise only *11.35* percent of U.S. newsroom employees today, according to a recent Editor and Publisher report. That's less than *half* the percentage of these minority groups in the general population.

But even that record looks good compared with the Web publishing industry, where many companies remain totally white. Startup companies are usually more concerned with trying to break even than with long-term social causes. And companies often argue that they don't have a large group of minority applicants to choose from in filling new jobs.

Most start-ups have to shift their priority in order to survive, so they are inclined to hire people they have worked closely with. In most cases, that pool of people didn't include many minorities.

I'm happy to report, at the time of this writing, the web has been proliferated with Black-oriented Web sites – like BlackAmericaWeb, BlackPlanet, Black Voice, and even my sites (*stevenefitch.com, imagine2morrow.com and e-marketplacemall.biz*).

http://BlackAmericaWeb.com
http://BlackPlanet.com
http://BlackVoice.com
http://stevenefitch.com
http://imagine2morrow.com
http://e-marketplacemall.biz

With the cost of doing business on the Internet decreasing, more and more ma-and-pa shops (small businesses) are coming online to offer the products and/or services to a global audience.

Basically, it boils down to preparation and making a stand to understand technology's importance. One doesn't have to know everything about technology, but to have an understanding will create a drive and interest. This eliminates fear! Dealing with this particular subject reminds me of the movie 'Total Recall' with Arnold Schwarzenegger, where those with a key will have all the oxygen, and those on the outside are either rebels or physically different somehow. In this analogy, it's minorities who seem not to have a key.

I'm happy to conclude that Ellington decided to open his business in San Francisco rather than Oakland, and have expanded his vision and technological services throughout California.

Changing our Priority to Bytes over Bling

Minorities need to change the order of priority of tangible *versus* intangible. Sure, there are items required to maintain a safe, healthy lifestyle, and those items should have a higher priority over technology. But as a whole, we get caught-up into the second tier of items that we miss the importance of education and its priority.

For example, marketing professionals have statistics that show Blacks and Hispanics favor entertainment brands, while technology and business media brands rank highest for Asians and affluent whites. In short, amusement, entertainment and athletics appear to have top priority among many in the minority community, while business media, education and future financial planning is geared towards non-blacks groups.

Even in our public schools, student-athletes receive more honor, praise and respect--and bigger trophies--than the scholars who work hard to excel academically. With that comes a tough conclusive statement that books and computers are not as valued as balls and hip-hop CDs. I would estimate that in Black households there is a stronger presence of more televisions, VCRs, DVD players, CD players, video games, high-end name brands and other amusement technology than personal computers. In addition, more magazines on image and entertainment than educational books. Many of these households are equipped with cable service and/or satellite dishes with all the premium channels, like HBO, ShowTime, and Black Entertainment Television, through which youth of America learn in part how to be Black. This is a tidal wave of ignorance, which must be countered to make significant headway in improving our schools.

There must be a radical change in the educational values in the minority community. It is a matter of values; a matter of priority; and now is the time to recognize, it's not about ability. [xvii]Dr. Ben Carson, the well-known pediatric neurosurgeon, has said *"the cause of the decline and fall of Greece, Rome and Egypt was that they became enamored with sports and entertainment and de-emphasized intellectual talents."* American Blacks are in the same state at the dawn of the 21st century. The kind of change required to improve this situation must come from within the community - starting with parents teaching their children the basics: *that the key to advancement and progress lies in education.*

Let me make one point perfectly clear, it's not that minorities don't want technology, or consistently don't want to have access to it – it's just not viewed as important. Sure,

---

Digital Divide: An Equation needing a Solution

technology is recognized as educational, but secondary education, like learning art and music.

Take the example of young intellectuals in our inner-city schools. Their peers consider this particular group as counter to the African American culture. Many are ridiculed and accused of *"acting white."* From a society standpoint, you are viewed as a nerd or geek if you are well versed with the use of technology within this demographic. And as for African-Americans, we pride ourselves in a reputation over just about anything. So, if we don't see an immediate advantage to stepping outside of the box and being different, there is no reason for us to pursue such things.

NOTE: Difference between a nerd

and a geek is, a geek gets paid.

A simple way to approach this problem is to try to re-prioritize your life and take a long look at society, and see how and where the trends are going. You can begin by doing the following:

- *check out the classifieds and observe what are the requirements of jobs opportunities*
- *talk to local small businesses about technology*
- *ask people in your community or church about technology*
- *if you have access to the Internet and email, join a online club (group) of your interest*
- *visit my site (http://stevenefitch.com/). More specifically, the **Ask the Tech** section, and review articles posted.*

So, go ahead and purchase a PC for your household (or business), and get trained on how to use it. If you are not sure what to look for when making your very first purchase of a computer, see the next section on ***Technology Divide***, or visit my web site, stevenefitch.com, then click on *Ask the Tech*. I've written several articles pertaining to this very subject.

http://stevenefitch.com/AsktheTech.htm

Education makes people easy to lead, but difficult to drive; easy to govern, but impossible to enslave. ~ Henry Peter Broughan

Case Study: Small Business use of Technology

Now that you have a computer, you still generate documents, you still keep them in folders, folders are kept within folders, and various people have access to them. Electronic filing systems can be vastly superior to paper filing systems if we remember to follow the business practices we used in a paper environment. Do you have documents on your computer or network server that are not in folders? How many? How does that compare to the number of documents you would have tossed into a file cabinet without filing? The good news is that at least (a) *the documents are listed alphabetically wherever they are stored,* and (b) *we can always "search" for them if we remember the name, or the software application, or when they were last modified.* Hhhhmmm. There must be a better way. You're right! And it's called a *common operating environment* (COE). In a business with a network environment, where a number of employees have access to a central data depository, you:

common operating environment

1) **Establish document-naming conventions**. As new documents are created, they are named in accordance with organizational policy. People looking for a document would have a good idea of the document name, even if someone else created it.

2) **Determine the file structure**. Folders within folders within folders. Organizing your information so that documents are easily located.

3) **Grant access as appropriate**. Security levels and edit rights, determining who can have access to what or not, when to permit "read-only" access, and who is authorized to make changes.

4) **Safeguard information**. Back-up systems, on and offsite, disaster recovery plans. If you do all of the above, provide training on the implementation, you will have established a COE. The benefits are enormous and immediate.

This technology enhancement is available right now from a wide variety of companies. Use a search engine of choice (i.e., Google™, Yahoo! ™, MSN™, Lycos™, Alta-Vista™, and Northern Light™) and enter *common operating environment (COE)*.

Using Databases to Work and Mine Data: Most of us couldn't imagine functioning without word processing software and spreadsheet software in our businesses. We all use e-mail and a lot of us can use presentation software, some more rudimentary than others. Yet, for some reason, the database software frequently goes unused in the small business.

Digitize, Digitize, Digitize: Maintaining our information in electronic form is critical to both the establishment of a COE and mining our data on an ongoing basis. Virtually all software applications allow for exporting data and importing data. So as long as you maintain your data electronically, you can take advantage of new software development in your industry without having to re-enter the information. Electronic files are easier to navigate and cheaper to maintain. Additional computers and memory are just less expensive than rent, file cabinets, and storage facilities.

You think about it: How far has your business moved along the learning continuum? Are you taking advantage of the latest technologies to codify the intellectual capital of your business? If you arrived at your office, and all your information OR all your money was gone, what would be more devastating to you? Now, compare how you safeguard your money with the way you safeguard your information. As you digitize your workflow, be sure you have adequate back-up systems with offsite storage for all-important information.

Digital Divide: An Equation needing a Solution

Chapter 3: Technology Divide

When computers (people) are networked, their power multiplies geometrically. Not only can people share all that information inside their machines, but also they can reach out and instantly tap the power of other machines (people), essentially making the entire network their computer. ~ Scott McNeely

More Americans than ever before have access to personal computers and the Internet. Never have so many Americans access to so much information and consumer goods as they do now. The Internet is changing how we communicate, shop, educate ourselves, get our news, and elect our leaders.

The software industry provides a battery of sophisticated products to the American consumer, available at prices driven down by stiff competition in the industry. Hardware is getting faster, software is getting better, and both are getting cheaper, while Internet Service Providers (ISPs) wage war with each other over rates, conveniences and services, making it easier and less expensive to get online. Indeed, the technology industry is thriving all over the world.

Internet Service Providers (ISP)

The first thing to remember about buying a computer is that anything you buy today will be obsolete tomorrow. Don't panic – this isn't a bad thing. . . buying technology is just like that. Just resign yourself to it, make a choice, and work with what you have. With that being said, it is also a good idea to buy the most expandable computer you can afford because it will serve you better and longer.

Today, almost any PC on the market can more than adequately handle such standard office chores as word processing and spreadsheets, as well as basic Internet functions like e-mail and general browsing. So, for $1000 or less, you can obtain a more than adequate PC.

The best way to pay for what you need, is to carefully consider what you want to do with your system now, and try to anticipate what might interest you next year. Specific applications call for certain types of hardware, whether at home or in the office. Continue reading to obtain a better understanding of items to look for when you are in the market for a computer.

The History of Computers

1936

Konrad Zuse builds the first freely programmable computer-Z1 Computer

John Atanasoff & Clifford Berry form ABC Computer

1942

1944

Howard Aiken and Grace Hopper build the Harvard mark 1 computer

John Presper Eckert & John W. Mauchly build ENIAC1

1946

1947

John Bardeen Walter Brattain & William Shockley invent the transistor

John Presper Eckert & John W. Mauchly invented the UNIVAC- first commercial computer.

1951

1953

International Business Machines (IBM) builds the IBM 701 EDPM Computers.

Jack Kilby & Robert Noyce developed the integrated circuit("the chip").

1958

Digital Divide: An Equation needing a Solution

Douglas Engelbart invents the computer mouse and windows.

1964

ARPANET (the original internet is created)

1969

UCSB was one of the four original sites of the ARPAnet, a forerunner of today's global internet.

1970

Intel invents the first available dynamic RAM chip

Illustration care of History of Computers

More on the History of Computers can be found by visiting http://www.computerhistory.org

Desktop Computers 101

What I have tried to do is cut through the *techno-talk* and explain the cutting edge information in its simplest form, and provide you with a budget driven computer.

A. Processor

The main factor in performance of your computer as well as the cost. The processor provides your computer with the necessary speed in order to process task. If you are thinking of writing a document or transmitting email, then a slower processor will serve you just fine. Now, on the other hand, if you are planning on running multimedia or gaming, look for a fast gigahertz (GHz) processor.

B. Hard Drive

This is used for storage of all computer data. In this case, more is absolutely better so purchase as much disk space as your wallet can handle, especially if this if going to be a family-used computer.

C. RAM stands for Random Access Memory (see Glossary for a more detailed definition). When addressing memory on your computer, the more you have, the faster you can access files. At the time of this writing, 512MB is the standard, but 1GB is an excellent option and highly recommended.

D. Optical Drive

This is better known as CD-ROM (or DVD) drive. These drives store and/or retrieve information from disk via laser technology. This item also allows you to share your personal creations such as photos, music, etc.

E. Sound

Having a good sound system on your computer nowadays will provide your lots versatility for listening to music, viewing movies, video games, chat sessions, etc.

F. Graphic Card

If processors and memory are everything, then a good graphic card is a close third. Graphic cards deliver realistic images for your viewing pleasure.

Digital Divide: An Equation needing a Solution

Major Computer Manufacturers

Acer™	Apple™	Dell™
(*http://www.acer.com*)	(*http://www.apple.com*)	(*http://www.dell.com*)
eMachines™	**Gateway™**	**Hewlett-Packard™**
(*http://www.emachines.com*)	(http://www.gateway.com)	*(merged with Compaq in 2004)* (*http://www.hp.com*)
IBM™	**Sony™**	**Toshiba™**
(*http://www.ibm.com*)	(*http://www.sony.com*)	(*http://www.toshiba.com*)

What are the most common uses of a computer?

- **Word Processor:** *the electronic manipulation of text characters. This includes creating documents such as letters, papers, reports, and mailing lists.*
- **Desktop Publishing:** *electronic page layouts for newsletters, magazines, flyers, and posters. This usually means the combinations of text and graphics.*
- **Database:** *the electronic manipulation of information. Being able to sort, organize, or find specific items out of large collections of information. This includes such things as mailing lists, inventories, and employee information.*
- **Spreadsheet:** *the electronic manipulation of numbers. Used for statistical analysis, accounting, expense reports, etc.*
- **Graphics:** *the electronic manipulation of graphical images. Used to edit still pictures, slides, scanned images, or full motion video.*
- **Audio / Video:** *the electronic manipulation of digital audio sounds and video streaming. Used in the manufacture of compact discs and digital tapes as well as overlaying existing video with a digital soundtrack.*
- **Communication:** *sending digital messages from one computer to another.*
- **E-mail:** *used in many offices around the world as a means of communication.*
- **Games:** *used at home to play a wide variety of video games.*

Unfortunately, it's darn near impossible for me, or any other technical person to prescribe to you the perfect purchase. Why? At the present time, technology is expanding even as I'm writing this book. At the time of this writing, the fastest available processor is 3.3 GHz. . . what is it today?

visit http://www.intel.com for up-to-date information

Five (5) items to consider when looking for a new, or even improve your existing computer:

- **Analyze your requirements vs. your pocket**
  Determine if you can afford the fastest processor available on the market.
- **Design and specify system you need – Windows vs. Macintosh**
  Both operating systems have pro's and cons. You will need to determine if you want to use Microsoft Windows platform, which is most commonly used around the world vs. Apple Macintosh platform. See next section for a closer comparison on (OS).
- **Select a manufacturer**
  If you select Apple Macintosh, well, your platform selections are limited to just one manufacturer. While on the other hand, the Microsoft platform, you have lots of choices to choose from (i.e. Dell™, Hewlett-Packard™, Gateway™, Toshiba™, IBM™, Acer™, Sony™, etc...).
- **Make the purchase**
  Once you have decided your need, how much you can afford, and which product best fits in line with your desire, go ahead and make the purchase.
- **After the purchase**
  At this point, let me be the first to welcome you into the computer age ☺. Inspect the package and make sure you have everything you are suppose to have, setup the computer and all of its peripherals, test that it works as expected, and most importantly, register. Registration provides you will your warranty as well as keeps you up-to-date on system updates and support.

The software used on PC's is broken down by categories. **Software** is a generic term referring to any computer application who's purpose is to help run the computer system. Most of it is responsible directly for controlling, integrating, and managing the individual hardware components of a computer system.

software

Digital Divide: An Equation needing a Solution

Operating Systems

An **operating system** (**OS**) is the system software responsible for the direct control and management of hardware and basic system operations. Additionally, it provides a foundation upon which to run application software, such as word processing programs and web browsers. Common OS available today are as follows:

operating systems

- *Microsoft® Windows™ 98 and Second Edition (SE)*

- *Microsoft® Windows™ 2000*

- *Microsoft® Windows™ Mobile*

- *Microsoft® Windows™ XP (Starter, Home, Professional)*

- *Apple® Macintosh™ (8, 9, X (Panther), Tiger)*

- *Microsoft® Windows™ 2003*

- *Microsoft® Windows™ Vista (Beta)*

- *Unix (Solaris, SCO, HP-UX)*

- *Linux (Red Hat, SuSE, Mandrake, Caldera)*

http://*microsoft.com*
http://*linux.com*
http://*redhat.com*
http://*apple.com*

If you are in the market for a computer, make sure you have these *basic* components:

- **Central Processing Unit**
- **Keyboard.**
- **Mouse**
- **Color monitor** *(it's nearly impossible to find a black and white monitor).*
- **Network Card**
- **Data / Fax modem.**
- **CD-ROM** *(compact disc-ROM)*
- **Printer**

Visit our glossary for further
explanation on the above components

At the time of this writing, here is a listing of popular product categories available today:

Internet Browsers

Internet™ Explorer - the latest Windows® XP Web browser technology from Microsoft
Netscape® - the latest official release of the Netscape web browser suite
Mozilla® Firefox – a cutting edge, next generation browser and able challenger to IE for browser supremacy
Opera® - the latest and best international Web browser — a Norwegian original
NCSA Mosaic - the original and once great web browser

http://microsoft.com/ie
http://netscape.com
http://mozilla.com/firefox/
http://opera.com
http://archive.ncsa.uiuc.edu/mosaic.html

Digital Divide: An Equation needing a Solution

Chat / Conferencing (Instant Messaging Tools)

Yahoo! ® Messenger with Voice - Yahoo's® chat solution for exchanging instant messages with your friends

AOL® Instant Messenger (AIM™) - AOL's® instant chat tool for sending free, private messages to your buddies

MSN® Messenger - Microsoft's® instant messaging service for sending free, private messages

MSN® Messenger for Mac® OS X - Microsoft's® instant messaging service for sending free, private messages

Google® Talk - a lightweight Jabber-based instant messaging client with voice capabilities
ICQ® - The all-new, streamlined Lite edition of ICQ® with Xtraz

Trillian® - a free, interoperable IM client with support for AIM™, ICQ, Yahoo!®, MSN®, and IRC

Gaim, - an open source, multi-protocol IM client that supports AIM™, ICQ, MSN® Messenger, Yahoo!®, IRC, Jabber, and more

Odigo - a unique IM client with a cool interface and powerful user search engine

Miranda IM, - a lean, mean multi-protocol IM machine that's fast, free, and easy to use

http://messenger.yahoo.com
http://aim.com
http://webmessenger.msn.com
http://google.com/talk
http://icq.com
http://ceruleanstudios.com
http://gaim.sourceforge.net
http://odigo.com
http://miranda-im.org

Chatting Tools

Microsoft™ NetMeeting® - Microsoft's™ entry into the Internet phone and conferencing battle
Skype® - Skype® lets you talk to anyone, anywhere for free over the Internet
Net2Phone® - Call anyone in the world from your PC — and save money while doing so
Active Worlds Browser - Your portal to an intriguing multi-user 3-Dimensional community

http://microsoft.com/windows/netmeeting
http://skype.com
http://net2phone.com

Desktop Utilities
Anti-Spam

Norton® AntiSpam™ 2005 - a solid anti-spam package bundled with the Norton Internet
Security suite

McAfee® SpamKiller™ 2005 - a powerful filter-based anti-spam tool that integrates with
McAfee's security suite

SPAMFighter - an effective, free (ad supported) anti-spam filter for Outlook and Outlook
Express

Cloudmark® Desktop for Outlook - reap the benefits of a spam-fighting community for
instant and highly accurate protection from spam

Cloudmark® Desktop for Outlook Express - reap the benefits of a spam-fighting
community for instant and highly accurate protection from spam

Spam Interceptor - a free web-based solution for efficiently eliminating spam

*http://symantec.com/**antispam***
***http://spamkiller**.com*
*http://**spamfighter**.com*
*http://**cloudmark**.com/*
http://si20.com

Anti-Virus

Norton® AntiVirus™ 2006
Symantec's extremely impressive virus scanner — the Y2K+5 edition

McAfee® VirusScan™ 2005, Version: 9.0
McAfee's excellent scanner with the new McAfee Security Center

Panda® Antivirus 2006, Version: 5.00.83
Threat-proof your PC with complete protection from known and unknown viruses,
hackers, spam, spyware, and other Internet threats

InoculateIT® Personal Edition, Version: 5.2.9
A completely free virus scanner that has unfortunately been discontinued

Inoculan® AntiVirus, Version: 6.0
Eliminate virus threats from shared files, e-mail, 'net downloads, and more

AVG Anti-Virus Free, Version: 7.0.344
A free scanner that combines real-time virus protection and e-mail scanning with free
virus definition updates and limited support

Digital Divide: An Equation needing a Solution

AVG Anti-Virus Plus Firewall, Version: 7.0
AVG's real-time Anti-Virus scanner paired with a powerful firewall for added security

F-Secure® Anti-Virus 2005, Version: 6.0
A very fast, very effective anti-virus program with Countersign Technology

Norman® Virus Control, Version: 5.70
A combination of NovaStor ThunderBYTE AV and Norman Virus Control

http://symantec.com
http://mcafee.com
http://pandasoftware.com
http://antivirus.ca.com
http://grisoft.com
http://f-secure.com
http://norman.com

Compression Tool

WinZip - An absolute must-have file compression/decompression utility

PKZIP - A timeless tool for efficiently compressing files, creating archives, and extracting files

WinRAR - A powerful archive manager and a formidable rival to WinZip

SecureZIP - PKZIP on steroids — a premium compression client with increased security and management capabilities

http://winzip.com
http://pkware.com
http://rarlab.com
http://pkware.com/business_and_developers/security

Utilities

Adobe® Acrobat Reader™ - An extremely useful product that allows you to read specialized documents over the Internet.

Yahoo! ® Desktop Search, - A new desktop search tool that capably searches through your PC's email messages, Office apps, PDF files, IE Web pages, songs, text files, and images

Google® Desktop Search, - A handy tool that enables desktop searching for files, emails, web history, and IM chats

MSN® Search Toolbar - A useful collection of toolbars for IE, Explorer, and Outlook that features both Web and desktop searching

Ask Jeeves® Desktop Search - Search for files and e-mails on your PC as you would search for information on Ask Jeeves

http://adobe.com/products/acrobat/readstep2.html
http://desktop.yahoo.com
http://desktop.google.com
http://toolbar.msn.com
http://sp.ask.com/en/docs/desktop/overview.shtml

Security

NOTE: *More on security of your computer and Internet in the next section.*

Norton® Internet Security™ 2006 -a comprehensive collection of security tools for total Internet protection

Norton® Internet Security™ 2005 AntiSpyware Edition - Internet security suite with new anti-spyware functionality

McAfee® Internet Security Suite 2005 - McAfee's® all-in-one security suite features McAfee® VirusScan™, Personal Firewall Plus, SpamKiller™, and Privacy Service

Panda® Internet Security 2006 - Threat-proof your PC with complete protection from known and unknown viruses, hackers, spam, spyware, and other Internet threats

F-Secure® Internet Security 2005 - An enticing collection of firewall, anti-virus, anti-spyware, spam filtering, and parental control components

PGP Freeware - The premier encryption software for ensuring the privacy of your e-mail

PGP Desktop - The premier encryption software for ensuring the privacy of your e-mail

Kaspersky™ Internet Security 2006 - an attractive, comprehensive security solution from the developers of AntiViral Toolkit Pro (AVP)

http://symantec.com
http://mcafee.com
http://pandasoftware.com
http://f-secure.com
http://pgp.com
http://kaspersky.com

Digital Divide: An Equation needing a Solution

System Utilities

CCleaner (Crap Cleaner), - a handy freeware tool that quickly and efficiently rids your system of needless junk as well as traces of your activity

X-Setup Pro- demystify your Windows Registry with this handy tool that simplifies nearly 1800 different registry settings

Security Task Manager - STM offers detailed, easy-to-understand information for all running processes on your PC

The Ultimate Troubleshooter - a valuable resource manager that can improve your PC's performance, startup times, and overall stability

http://ccleaner.com
http://x-setup.net
http://snapfiles.com/reviews/ Security_Task_Manager/securitytask.html
http://answersthatwork.com/TUT_pages/TUT_information.htm

Multimedia

Audio

ITunes™ - a platform which allows users to listen to hundred of thousands of audio selections ranging from music, video ,books, etc…

AOL®Media Player (AMP) - a standalone media app that will play your CDs, music and video files, and AOL Radio stations as well as burn CDs

Rhapsody® - a subscription-based music service that features an on-demand catalog, 100+ radio stations, and CD burning capabilities

Notify CD Player - a small but powerful freeware CD player with built-in CDDB support

ToolVox - streaming audio tool serves high-quality voice content from any web server

MusicMatch® Jukebox - jumping' jukebox! A digital audio MP3 player, CD ripper, and CD burner

Winamp® - by far the best MP3 audio player on the 'net — and it's free!

Audio Xtract Pro - an affordable approach to building your MP3 library ... legally

Audioactive - high-quality, real-time audio on-demand streaming for the web

MidiGate - a full-scale MIDI player that also functions as a web helper app

http://apple.com/itunes
http://stream.info.aol.com/aolmedia.html
http://rhapsody.com
http://rjamorim.com/rrw/voxware.html
http://musicmatch.com
http://winamp.com
http://audioactive.com
http://freedownloadscenter.com/Multimedia_and_Graphics/ MIDI_Players_and_Editors/Midigate.html

Graphics

Adobe® Creative Suite™ - the full versions of Adobe® Photoshop CS2™, Illustrator CS2™, InDesign CS2™, GoLive CS2™, and Acrobat 7™ in one package

Adobe® Photoshop™ - the premier image editing software package — nothing else comes close

Adobe® Photoshop Elements™ - a trimmed-down version of Adobe® Photoshop™ for the budget-conscious consumer

Paint Shop Pro X™, - an excellent, inexpensive graphics app comparable to Adobe® Photoshop™

Macromedia® Fireworks MX®™ - everything you need to create, optimize, and animate cool Web graphics

Ulead® GIF Animator®™- an easy to use, powerful app for creating animated GIFs with special effects

Ulead® SmartSaver Pro™ - a GIF/JPEG/PNG image optimizer specifically designed for webmasters

GIF Construction Set™ - a useful tool for adding flavor (and animation) to your GIF images
LView Pro 2005 - a graphics app that excels at creating Web galleries and slide shows

SnagIt - a feature-laden screen capture tool for easily copying and sharing any image, text, or video

http://adobe.com/products/creativesuite
http://adobe.com
http://corel.com
http://adobe.com/products/fireworks
http://ulead.com
http://mindworkshop.com/alchemy/gifcon.html
http://cws.internet.com/file/11662.htm
http://snagit.com

Digital Divide: An Equation needing a Solution

Video

Windows Media Player™ - the scintillating successor to NetShow and Microsoft's® Media Player™

RealPlayer® - next generation real-time audio, video, and Flash on-demand multimedia

Real Alternative™ - a simple yet powerful, ad-free multimedia player that can handle a wide range of formats

AOL® Media Player (AMP) – a standalone media app that will play your CDs, music and video files, and AOL Radio stations as well as burn CDs

QuickTime™ for Windows™ - a multimedia viewer/plug-in for playing QuickTime™ and other A/V files

Zoom Player - Zoom's ambitious effort to support every form of multimedia may just deliver

MPEGPlay - an extremely dated freeware player for viewing MPEG video files

http://microsoft.com/windows/windowsmedia
http://real.com
http://free-codecs.com/download/Real_Alternative.htm
http://stream.info.aol.com/aolmedia.html
http://apple.com/quicktime/download
http://inmatrix.com
http://cws.internet.com/file/11426.htm

Further Assistance with Purchasing a Computer

There are a number of venues available to provide assistance to you when purchasing a computer.

- **DELL®**
  (http://dell.com)
- **Gateway®**
  (http://gateway.com)
- **Apple®**
  (http://apple.com)

- **Best Buy®**
  (http://bestbuy.com)
- **Circuit City®**
  (http://circuitcity.com)
- **Inexpensive solutions**
  (Wal-Mart®, CDW®)

- **Charitable Organizations**

At the end of the day, we must re-prioritize our day-to-day habits and allow ourselves to get comfortable on some level of using technology. For more on this subject, visit the section on *Solving the Digital Divide.*

Safe guarding your Computer

Securing your home computer is not a trivial task. It may very well be one of the most important tasks you take on *post*-purchasing your computer. Of course, a computer is nothing more than an electric appliance with multiple, external connection points, but it's still an investment. Do you remember your first car? Sure it was beater, but it was yours and you did everything you could to keep it clean and safe. You even went out and purchase The Club™ didn't you? Why? Because you wanted to protect your baby. Well, the same concept is true. You need to secure and protect your computer from external elements.

FOUR EASY STEPS TO PROTECT YOUR WINDOWS PC AND YOURSELF:

1. Update Your Operating System

No software is perfect. Unfortunately, when it comes to operating systems, there are security vulnerabilities that can be exploited. The good news: updating your operating system is relatively easy to accomplish.

For example, to update Microsoft® Windows™ operating system, either (1) go to http://windowsupdate.microsoft.com or (2) go to Internet Explorer™, click on "tools," then click on "Windows update" and follow the instructions. You should update Web browsers, such as Internet Explorer, as well.

2. Install & Update Virus Protection Software

With the prevalence of computer viruses, having virus protection on your machine is a MUST. Some virus protection software's offer automatic update, but only if you have a full-time Internet connection (DSL or cable). If you don't have full-time Internet or your virus protection software does not automatically update, then you need to update by following the software manufacturer's instructions.

3. Install & Update Spyware Protection Software

Spyware/adware exploit holes in browser security and install unwanted software on your computer that over time can slow down your computer. While most of these intrusions are just nuisances, many are actually gathering information on your Internet habits and transmitting it to a third party. A Web user is left with few options. Either you increase browser security settings and severely limit your use of the Internet or obtain a spyware protection program, such as "Spybot: Search and Destroy." For many reasons, obtaining a spyware program is a better idea. You might want to try using one of the alternate browsers (like FireFox-- http://www.mozilla.org) as they are not as frequently targeted by spyware.

4. Install a Personal Firewall

Most hacking dangers come from scripts run by individuals searching for a specific set of criteria--usually open ports on random computers that they can use later to launch attacks. The danger is magnified by computer users with DSL/cable or other "always on" connections, especially if they leave their computer on all the time. A personal firewall will help protect you. In most cases, a firewall will also allow the user to dictate which programs can and cannot access the Web.

The sad fact is that the more we use computers and the Internet, the more ways are going to be found for them to be used against us. The best way to fight back is to educate yourself and set up good computer protection habits. Update your operating system and your Internet browsers regularly. Add virus and spyware protection and be vigilant about keeping them updated. Add a firewall, especially if you use an "always on" connection.

Finally, if you use the Internet and have difficulty dealing with these four steps, I suggest you seek advice from family or friends because these *four* steps are crucial to safeguarding your computer from intrusions.

Support Assistance

I'm certain if you purchased a new computer, you have a limited warranty and support on the product. In most cases, you may have even purchased an additional support package, which is definitely worth it. As you can imagine, there are number of companies available that can provide you with additional assistance, but for a charge:

- *Geeks-on-call™ - http://geeksoncall.com*
- *Best Buy® - http://bestbuy.com*
- *CompUSA® - http://compusa.com*
- *CDW® - http://cdw.com*
- *Check with your local communities or organizations for additional assistance, or maybe even your local listings*

"Emotion without information breeds fear." - Anonymous

Case Study: Do You Want A Receipt?

On my way to work, I needed to get some cash so I could have some W.A.M. (*walk around money*). As many of you already know, most banks are closed until 9:00am, so in order to gain access to my money, I turned to my 24 hour / 7 day a week, high-tech, present day banker representative – Ms. A.T.M. Yeah, she's female especially in my house and for good reason too but that's another article all together... Any hoot, in order to gain access to Ms. A.T.M. I stopped at a local satellite branch for my bank, which will remain nameless - no reason to give them FREE press. At the satellite location, you must use your 3 3/8" by 2 1/8" bank card which holds the key to speak to her as well as the necessary security measures to ensure you are who you say you are, at anytime of the day, as well as at any location around the world.

Once my security clearance was approved, the door clicked and I was able to gain access to Ms. A.T.M, my high-tech, present day banker representative. I entered the door, I slowly walk up to her – humble and hoping she was operational. I inserted my bank card in the appropriate slot and began my transaction, which went like this:

English or Spanish? *I pressed English*

Enter your password: *beep beep beep beep;*

What is your transaction? *withdrawal*

From which account? *whichever one has money*

How much? *80 dollars – that's a good total for some W.A.M.*

Processing your request...

Since I went to my banks' ATM, I wasn't charged a service fee.

Flip flip flip flip - the sound of four twenties coming out of the machine

Take your money...

Do you want a receipt? *Yes*

Would you like another transaction? *No*

Transaction complete

Please take your card.

Digital Divide: An Equation needing a Solution

Beep Beep Beep

Now, I shared all of that to say, that *back in the day*, my mother's experience would have been totally different.

First and foremost, she couldn't go before heading to work unless she made prior arrangements to come in late. So, in this case, let's say she made these arrangements - she would have had to wait until the bank opened at 9:00am. Once she arrived at the bank

- she would have had to fill out a withdrawal slip, then
- wait in line for the teller, then
- watch as the teller raises her eyebrows as she admires the meager balance in her account, then
- receive the money she wanted,
- of course, offer her a service, knowing she didn't need, want nor afford it, then
- smile and greet her neighbors in line.

Now you might say, this sounds like a more civilized and humane way to start your day off, but is it *efficient? And what are the results of this change?* Technology has allowed our society the following advantages:

- More convenient for people like me, more access to my money.
- More privacy in my banking - fewer tellers looking at my account.
- Fewer employees on the bank's payroll.
- More time to focus on other business issues / transactions during a given day.

Why is the experience different today than it was years back?

Because networks of computers and easy-to-use software have enabled banks to deliver its retail services in a more efficient and more convenient way.

Unfortunately, banking is a "*necessary evil*" that can take a large chunk out of already busy schedules. As stated, visiting a branch can be time consuming while using an ATM (or even banking online), by its nature, can automate many of these processes, saving you time and, in many cases, money. With the use of technology, you can access your account and do your banking when (and where) it is convenient for you. In addition, most banks allow you to bank by phone as well. In this case, you are never too far away from accessing information about your money.

Some *Fun* Facts About ATM Machines

- *ATM customers spend an average of 30 to 35% more than non-ATM customers.*
- *60% of Americans ages 25-34 and 51% ages 25-49 use ATM machines 8 times a month, withdrawing an average of $55.00 per transaction.*
- *In 2001, there were 8.3 billion ATM transactions in the United States, while in 2006, there were over 10.1 billion ATM transactions.*
- *Bank ATMs average 6,400 transactions per month.*
- *The most popular day for ATM usage is Friday.*
- *Among people that use both credit and debit cards, debit cards are used most often. 5.9 times per month versus 5.1 times per month.*
- *Independent studies show that cash retention among large retailers is 30-33%. Retention among smaller retailers is 35-40%.*
- *Nightclubs are seeing 70-80% of the dispensed cash staying at the club.*
- *Retail location ATM machines that dispense $20.00 bills increase store sales by over 8%.*

Digital Divide: An Equation needing a Solution

Conclusion

The way we handle daily task from financial transactions to pumping gas to making simple purchases of such items as books, has changed dramatically over the years. Using today's technological edge, a person's time is used more efficiently, with faster, easier, less expensive, and more convenience than ever before. In this particular case study, I dealt with a computer - an ATM, which is actually a computer connected to a nationwide network, running easy-to-use software. The use of such computers, networks, and software enables the industries - retail banking, gasoline distribution, and bookselling - to be conducted in much more convenient and profitable manner for all parties.

Needless to say, basic interface with the consumers is completely different than ever before.

- *Consumers' deal much more directly with the business with fewer live human intermediaries.*
- *For the business owner, there's more capital investment in computers and networks, balanced by less expense for labor and people in the front lines -- much less.*
- *And with today's cheap capital and expensive labor, it's a foregone conclusion that these trends will continue.*
- *And with consumers demanding more convenience, and wanting to conduct their business whenever and wherever they have a free moment, you can be sure that the market will drive all the banks to adopt the new model. It's the only way they'll be able to survive in business.*

In fact, almost more basic transactions occur at an ATM than in the lobby of a bank. Other industries that affect the way we carry out the business of our day-to-day lives, are also beginning to change (or have successfully made the conversion) as a result of the power and ubiquity of computers and networks. Let's look at a few that are just beginning to change, and ask yourself:

How is it different from the old way?

What is causing the change?

What disappears?

• *Stamps and tracking packages (usps.gov & ups.com)*	• *Television (NBC.com, ABC.com, BET.com)*
• *Stock (etrade.com, scottrade)*	• Radio (npr.org)
• *Groceries (peapod.com)*	• *Shopping (ebay.com)*
• *News (cnn.com)*	• *Education (keller.edu, phoenix.edu, imagine2morrow.com)*
• *Newspaper (usatoday.com, nytimes.com)*	• *Restaurant (Lou Malnati Pizza with next day delivery)*

These are efficient, responsive, effective, faster, cheaper, more convenient, and available to more people in more places at any time. So, in a free market, they will prevail. No area of business is untouched, unaffected. They are changing, inexorably, and quickly.

In short, technology has allowed us to live in an era of instant… from instant coffee to microwavable foods to common every day task as stated in this article. Technology can, and will continue to provide us with a glimpse into life as the Jetson's lived but deploying technology for technology sake isn't advantageous.

The face of these industries has changed considerably over the years and to be competitive you had to change or be left behind. For additional case study's on the subject, please visit my web site

http://www.sefitch.com/Archives/Do%20you%20want%20a%20receipt.pdf (or

http://www.sefitch.com/news.htm)

Digital Divide: An Equation needing a Solution

Chapter 4: Educational Divide

In the space program, I've had the opportunity to learn about a number of different fields, to be involved in technology that's right on the edge, pushing to see where it can go. ~ Mae C. Jemison

Technology is making a significant, positive impact on education. Highlights of these findings are as follows:

- *Educational technology has demonstrated a significant positive effect on society. Positive effects have been found for all major subject areas, from preschool to higher education, and for both regular education and special needs students. Evidence suggests that interactive video is especially effective when the skills and concepts to be learned have a visual component and when the software incorporates a research-based instructional design. Use of online telecommunications for collaboration across classrooms in different geographic locations has also been show to improve academic skills.*
- *Educational technology has also been found to have positive effects on student attitudes toward learning and on student self-concept. Students felt more successful in school were more motivated to learn and have increased self-confidence and self-esteem when using computer-based instruction. This was particularly true when the technology allowed learners to control their own learning.*
- *The specific student population, the software design, the teacher's role, how the students are grouped, and the level of student access to the technology influence the level of effectiveness of educational technology. Furthermore, students trained in collaborative learning had higher self-esteem and student achievement.*
- *Introducing technology into the learning environment has been shown to make learning more student-centered, to encourage cooperative learning, and to stimulate increased teacher/student interaction.*
- *Positive changes in the learning environment brought about by technology are more evolutionary than revolutionary. These changes occur over a period of years, as teachers become more experienced with technology. In addition, courses for which computer-based networks were use increased student-student and student-teacher interaction, increased student-teacher interaction with lower-performing students, and did not decrease the traditional forms of communication used. Many students who seldom participate in face-to-face class discussion become more active participants online. Furthermore, research has shown that greater student cooperation and sharing and helping behaviors occurred when students used computer-based learning that had students compete against the computer rather than against each other.*

Digital Divide: An Equation needing a Solution

Educational trends

A further breakdown of educational trends finds that those with college degrees, the rate of PC literacy exceed 97.0%. At the other end, those with only some high school education have the lowest penetration rates, particularly in central city areas.

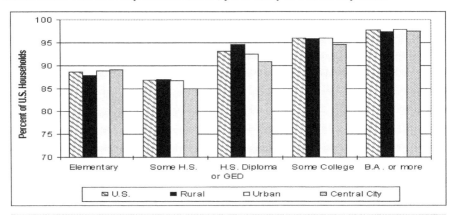

	U.S.	Rural	Urban	Central City
Elementary	88.6	87.9	88.9	89.1
Some H.S.	86.8	87.0	86.7	85.0
H.S. Diploma or GED	93.2	94.7	92.5	90.9
Some College	96.0	95.9	96.0	94.7
B.A. or more	97.8	97.4	97.9	97.6

Not surprisingly, school finance is another important part of the picture. In most parts of the country, schools are still financed by property taxes. Wealthy areas have large tax bases and can have robust technology budgets, while less affluent areas cannot afford adequate technology resources. Unless other funding mechanisms are found, school districts in low-income areas will neither be able to provide adequate technology to students nor the trained teachers to instruct them. More than ever, what you earn is a product of what you learn. In an economy quickly becoming information-based, it is technology know-how that is most needed for people to emerge from the lowest income brackets.

The bottom line is access to technology, which is directly linked to income level. Even though computers have become more and more affordable, many people still do not have the means to buy a computer. Households with incomes of $75,000 or more are nine times as likely to have a computer at home, and 20 times more likely to have access to the Internet than those at the lowest income levels. Currently, over 60 percent of people with college degrees use the Internet, compared to fewer than 7 percent of those with an elementary school education or less.

Thus, as stated before, the increased competition among PC-providers and lower costs of manufacturing have resulted in PCs selling for below $500. Additionally, the increasing use of other Internet-accessing devices, such as televisions, handheld computers, and Internet phones, should further invigorate competition among manufacturers and reduce prices for consumers.

While competition has made computers and the Internet increasingly affordable, these technologies still remain beyond the budget of many American households. When asked why they lacked Internet access, a significant portion of households (36.8%) responded that it was too expensive.

Competition is a significant answer to providing affordable access to computers and the Internet, but it is not the total solution. It is highly unlikely that, in the foreseeable future, prices will fall to the point where most homes will have computers and Internet access. Unfortunately, as a result, a *digital divide* may continue to exist at home between the information rich and the information poor. Given the great advantages accruing to those who have access, it is not economically or socially prudent to idly wait for the day when

Digital Divide: An Equation needing a Solution

most, if not all, homes can claim connectivity. Part of the short-term answer lies in providing Internet access at *community access centers* (CACs), such as schools, libraries, and other public access facilities. In addition, we should look to other community-based organizations that can help achieve these goals -- traditional community centers, churches, credit unions, housing projects, senior centers, museums, fire and police stations, and more.

What can people do now?

While many Americans are embracing computers and the Internet, there are many others who do not realize that technology is here to stay. When was the last time you made a call to a utility company, or to your bank and received a human voice without pressing an additional button on the phone?

Technology has great promise and by leveling the playing field, it can remove barriers rather than create new ones. Without decisive and direct measures, the dangers of the *digital divide* will only become larger, as our economy increasingly depends on skilled employees and computer-savvy consumers. Fortunately, the solutions are many, and to date, many players are coming forward to narrow the ***digital divide***. Inner city community organizations, large corporations, colleges and universities, and government agencies are all taking steps to level the technological playing field. Examples of community technology centers are springing up in cities is as follows:

- *Nationally recognized community-based organizations, such as Boys and Girls Club and Urban League, are promoting technology education by providing free access and after school programs.*
- *Fortune 500 companies are partnering with grass root organizations to provide resources to help fulfill the need for training and education.*
- *Large technology corporations are partnering with public institutions such as libraries to wire facilities, and the federal "e-rate" program pays for Internet access, enabling many poor and rural communities to wire classrooms cheaply.*

Steps, such as these, are a start toward making technology a unifying presence and an agent for social mobility, rather than a divisive force in our society.

Again, simply owning a computer and subscribing to the Internet does not bring you the advantage of "*connectedness*" - it's what you do with the computer that counts. Most of the students of today are on the upside of *digital divide*. Many students have been exposed to computers either at school, a friend's house, the library, etc. . . and their use of the computer sounds like this:

- *All my music is on the computer; I have over 2,000 MP3's files that I have downloaded. Plus, I make my own CD's.*
- *I can watch movies on my PC*
- *I can keep in touch with my friends with email and instant messaging, as well as surf the web.*
- *I keep up to date on the latest video games and industry news*

I posed a question in the previous section inquiring will any of these same students do better in school than their non-computer owning peers? I recognize, in advance, answering this question is somewhat complex, but I will say only if they (students) are limited to their digital resources. These kinds of activities will not make them better writers, historians, scientists, or mathematicians. Using email and instant messenger may make them faster at the keyboard, and video games may develop their motor skills, but these do not translate to a big advantage in the academic curriculum.

Broad surveys of high school and college students' use of computer find that their top activities are email and entertainment. Even if every student were issued a free computer upon entry into kindergarten, if they continued in this pattern of usage, the effects on their learning would be slim.

One of the main items the *digital divide* should fear is the split between the educational and entertainment uses of the new technologies. If these new powerful tools in the hands of our young people end up focused on trivial pursuits, they become defined by the society as grown-up Game boys (or gamers), and if we find ourselves as educators on the wrong side of the divide, we will have lost a major battle with the forces of ignorance. In order for this generation to take advantage of the digital equity available today, schools and teachers, as well as parents must ensure that educational forces occupy computers. Teachers have to learn how to give homework assignments that force students to use the

Digital Divide: An Equation needing a Solution

technology for serious writing, deep historical research, sophisticated science, and new ways of looking at math. Making sure that students' time with technology is taken up with worthwhile pursuits. Sure, students use instant messaging and email, as well as listen to music on their computers, but that's not the chief usage. In fact, today in many poorer areas of Chicago, you will find more of this demographic mastering the use of technology than in the wealthier computer-owning suburbs on the other side of the *digital divide*. They will as a result of this know how to use a computer to find worthwhile facts and interesting opinions, to use a variety of digital tools for analysis and thinking, and be able to present their ideas in the most appropriate electronic form. This, ultimately, can and should make them better students; more computerize in college courses, and more fitted to the world of work, than their well-to-do counterparts.

The *digital divide* is real, but it goes far deeper than who have a computer and who does not. It's a divide stretched by the forces of entertainment, which is pulling in one direction, and of education which is pulling in the other direction. As educators, we have a responsibility to do as much as we can to provide assignments and expectations that attract the computers to our side of the mountain.

 *Now what?*

What can we do to resolve the Education Divide?

In my humble opinion, we have *two* choices: we can continue to look at technology as an extra resource to assist people in their day-to-day lifestyles and/or tasks, or we can take full advantage of the new technologies by accommodating the way we teach and practice business task to reflect the advancements of technology.

Here are some additional possibilities:

- *Move up the taxonomy.* With facts and information at our fingertips, business people and students alike can spend more time becoming familiar with higher-order skill development by comparing, contrasting and evaluating various assignments.
- *Develop challenging assignments.* Anticipate the newly expanded access that your students enjoy, and work it into the lesson. If *George Phillips Bond* was alive today, he might begin his lesson with a question: *How many planets are there?* Then he would let his students go online and find the answer(s) and engage in a thought-provoking discussion on the planets and solar system.

http://members.leapmail.net/~ericj/bond.html

- *Allow teachers to really learn as they go.* A classroom should be open to *new* information, which will present challenges – students will collect and confront ideas that some teachers may never been faced with before. To survive in this *new* environment, teachers need to be ready to learn right along with the students.
- *And finally, begin to work outside of the box.* There is nothing wrong with structure and firm commitment to standardizing the basics of education, but allow for administration to improvise and expand their learn practice can work in a proactive manner. It can allow teachers to develop a strong, highly motivated curriculum that can allow student-teacher lines communication development, as well as bring more excitement and energy to the classroom.

Despite its crucial connection to economics and social development, teacher training is often uneven, protracted, or unsupported. In addition, teachers are rarely included in educational policy change or significant decision-making. Teachers are not just a resource for children; they have to be looked upon as key individuals to development tomorrow's curriculum.

In closing, don't blame the technology for the loss of control in and around the classroom. Instead, take some time to think things through in order to capitalize on its capabilities and move the level of learning up a notch.

While we teach our children all about life, our children teach us what life is all about. ~
Angela Schmidt

Case Study: Safeguard your Personal Computer

In the aftermath of the September 11 terrorist attacks, businesses and home PC users are consciously thinking more about protecting themselves as well as existing data obtained like never before. Despite the types of physical attacks demonstrated on September 11, PC's are constantly under some type of attack. In a nutshell, a personal computer connected to the Internet without a firewall can be hijacked in just a few minutes by automated hacker "Bots". The only way to make your computer 100% secure is to turn it off, or disconnect it from the Internet. The real issue is how to make your computer 99% secure when it is connected. Not having protection is like leaving your car running with the doors unlocked, windows down, and the keys in it, which a thief might interpret as "please steal me". Stated another way, when was the last time you handed a stranger your wallet and encouraged them to take your social security card, driver's license, cash and credit cards? Locking a car, using a "club" or installing a security system makes stealing a car more difficult. Internet security and privacy products provide adequate protection by making it difficult for "outlaws" to take control of your computer and rip you off.

The bottom line, at a minimum, is any computer connected to the Internet needs to have all current patches to its operating system and browser installed as well as personal firewall, antivirus and anti-spyware software. A more complete solution is taking a layered approach to protect your security and privacy as follows:

- **First line of defense** -- Choose an **Internet service provider** and/or an **email service** that offers online (server side) virus and spam email filters.
- **Second line of defense** -- Install a **wired** or **wireless** hardware router with a built in firewall between your modem and your computer or network. Also consider using a **broadband gateway** offering a combination of hardware and security software.
- **Third line of defense** -- Use a **security software suite** or a collection of individual software products including, at a minimum, **personal firewall, anti-spyware,** and **anti-virus** products. Also consider using **anti-Trojan, anti-spam, anti-phishing,** and **privacy** software. Please note that cost is not an issue since there is good **security freeware** available.

Important Tips

- Update and **tighten** Windows before installing new security software.
- To avoid conflicts, do not use two software firewalls or two anti-virus products at the same time. Completely uninstall one before installing another.
- You can and should use a hardware firewall and a software firewall at the same time.
- A security software suite or broadband gateway may be supplemented with individual products as needed to add or strengthen a feature. Also, if you are given the option, do not install features that you do not need or will not use.
- After installing any security software, **immediately** check for updates at the vendor's website.
- After installing a firewall, use an online **testing** service to make sure that it is working correctly.

Treat your password like your toothbrush. Don't let anybody else use it, and get a new one every six months. Clifford Stoll

Chapter 5: Solving the Divide

Technology presumes there's just one right way to do things. . . ~ Robert M. Pirsig

In order to resolve the ***digital divide,*** we must look at all aspects of it. Thus, a *one solution fits all* approach isn't the answer. What may be good in Chicago and New York, may not work in Dallas or Los Angeles (and vice-versa). But as a whole, we must first recognize and agree that there is a gap between the *haves* and the *have-nots*, and attempt to break down the barriers to eliminate the gap.

Training and education are very important parts of the effort to close the ***digital divide***. As previously stated, community access centers (CACs) -- such as schools, libraries, and other public access points – have played an important role. In the late nineties, data demonstrated that CACs are particularly well used by those groups who lack access at home or at work. These same groups, such as those with lower incomes and education levels, certain minorities, and the unemployed, are also using the Internet at higher rates to search for jobs or take courses. Providing public access to the Internet will help these groups advance economically, as well as provide them the technical skills to compete professionally in today's digital economy. Establishing and supporting these CACs, will also help ensure that all Americans can access new technologies. In the Information Age, access to computers and the Internet is becoming increasingly vital. It is in everyone's interest to ensure that no American is left behind.

The following examples highlight the breadth of the ***digital divide*** today:

- *Those with a college degree are more than eight times as likely to have a computer at home, and nearly sixteen times as likely to have home Internet access, as those with an elementary school education.*
- *A high-income household in an urban area is more than twenty times as likely as a rural, low-income household to have Internet access.*
- *A child in a low-income White family is three times as likely to have Internet access as a child in a comparable Black family, and four times as likely to have access as children in a comparable Hispanic household.*
- *A wealthy household of Asian/Pacific Islander descent is nearly thirteen times as likely to own a computer as a poor Black household, and nearly thirty-four times as likely to have Internet access.*
- *Finally, a child in a dual-parent White household is nearly twice as likely to have Internet access as a child in a White single-parent household; while a child in a dual-parent Black family is almost four times as likely to have access as a child in a single-parent Black household.*

The above data reveals that the ***digital divide*** -- the disparities in access to telephones, personal computers (PCs), and the Internet across certain demographic groups -- still exists and, in many cases, has *widened significantly*. The gap for computers and Internet access has generally grown larger by categories of education, income, and race.

The disparity based on race/origin is affected by income level. At the highest income level ($75,000 or higher), there is virtually *no difference* among household penetration rates (see chart below). At the lowest income level (less than $15,000) the disparities are pronounced: American Indians/Eskimos/Aleuts (72.3%), Blacks (78.1%), and Hispanics (81.9%) have the lowest penetration rates, compared to Asians/Pacific Islanders (90.9%) and Whites (89.1%).

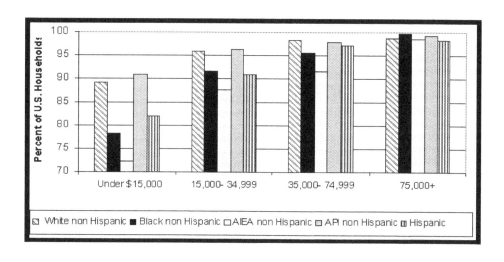

Digital Divide: An Equation needing a Solution

Approach 1: Teachers

Teachers are being asked to use technology in the classroom and to make sure they have everything they need. In most cases, recommendations will begin with hardware and software issues / requirements. But, to out right recommend something, in this case, is not an easy answer. All things being equal, I recommend teachers receive *six* things: *access, encouragement, inspiration, organization, underpinnings, and sometimes youth.* More details on these *six* items can be found on my web site: http://www.stevenefitch.com/digitaldivide/approach1.pdf.

Approach 2: Corporate Involvement

Various companies are providing solutions ranging from access to technology, education, financial assistance/donations and actual hardware/products. I have chosen to highlight *three* projects from companies helping to provide access to technology from *AT&T*™, *AOL*™, *and Microsoft*™ below:

- AT&T™ has initiated several programs in the effort to spawn technology centers for educational purposes, including collaboration with the NAACP. The National Urban League and the Community Technology Centers' Network have begun nationwide Community Technology Centers that offer under-resourced communities access to technology. One of these programs, the Los Angeles Neighborhood Technology Center has established twenty-five neighborhood-based technology centers and helps to support the Los Angeles County Office of Education's Technology for Learning Initiative. AT&T™ also provides resources through an AT&T™ Learning Network and by supporting the Puente Learning Center in South Central Los Angeles.

- AOL™, through the AOL Foundation, has also been active in charitable technology programs. The company has established the AOL™ Rural Telecommunications Leadership Awards, a partnership with the National Center for Small Communities, which seeks to reduce the *digital divide* by recognizing telecommunications in rural areas. AOL™ has also partnered with the Benton Foundation to create helping.org a nonprofit Web site that offers services and volunteer information to communities. The site has enabled user contributions to more than 620,000 US charities.

- Microsoft™ and the Bill and Melinda Gates Foundation have rewarded multiple grants to organizations including the Connected Learning Community, Working Connections, Higher Education for Minorities, and the TRIO programs. Microsoft™ has made donations of more than $5 million in funds and over $1 million in software resources to establish technology centers in Boys & Girls Clubs around the nation. The Gates Foundation has donated similar funds and software to offer technology access at libraries in low-income communities.

In addition, at the time of this writing, a host of high-tech giants, such as Yahoo! ™, Advanced Micro Devices (AMD) and Radio Shack® have announced plans for bridging the *digital divide*. They are partnering together to provide low-priced computers to the market. Right now, the devices will be called *Personal Internet Communicator*. The idea was to make something simple, durable and reliable for approximately $300 that will provide people simple PC-like chores, such as surfing the Internet, checking e-mail, writing simple documents, etc... Another innovation geared towards bridging the *digital divide* gap is an *always-connected* campaign where inexpensive laptops are always connected to the Internet. This innovation has a chance to change the way we read newspapers, watch TV or even listen to the radio and hear news from around the world. This campaign hopes to eliminate the social problem of the *digital divide* and make hardware even more affordable at the PC level, as well as at the access point (i.e., DSL and cable modem). From here, the society must continue to convenience people to buy computers and go online, and make this a priority.

Approach 3: Tools for Bridging the Gap

Here are some ideas provided by US Department of Education: *Office of Technology,* which offers basic tips on how to bridge the ***digital divide*** through the development of a community project. You can further explore a *"Tool Kit"* white paper for detailed information to assist in closing the gap:

Information Gathering	Coalition Building	Goal Setting	Establishing Evaluation Criteria
Identifying Resources	Planning	Grant Writing	

While it doesn't *guarantee* the success of a project, the *"Tool Kit"* provides many useful tips to help you get started on the road to success!

http://www.ed.gov/Technology/tool_kit.html

A New Kind of Learning:

Virtual Learning, Telementoring & e-Coaching

Instructor-led e-learning courses are similar to classroom-style courses in that they are interactive, feature specific start and end dates, usually require textbooks, and provide the same levels of academic and professional credit. You can experience a high level of instructor/class interaction within set start and end dates to help keep you focused and motivated. You receive personalized instructor feedback, and share insights and information with fellow learners.

There are many programs providing technology specific job training and family tutoring. Examples include:

- **PowerUP**, a collaboration of 12 nonprofit organizations have launched a multimillion dollar initiative to help ensure that America's underserved young people acquire the skills, experiences and resources they need to succeed. AOL has pledged 100,000 free Internet access accounts for this purpose.

- **CitySkills.org** (http://cityskills.org), an organization that works with community-based programs to offer training for high-demand Web related jobs to underserved urban adults.

- **Educate.com** (http://educate.com), provides a unique approach to learning. They begin by identifying your child's specific needs with a Sylvan Skills Assessment, then they create a personalized program just for your child, then work with each child individually, so your child receives the specific help he or she needs.

- *Imagine2morrow* (http://imagine2morrow.com), an innovative, nonprofit (pending) corporation in the state of Illinois that provides a learning program that looks to bridge the technological gap between the so-called *digital divide*. In order to accomplish our objective, we offer a variety of programs that serve community members of every age and background, as well as developed an online learning (*e-learning*) solution for people of all ages at an affordable cost.

Other things that can be done right now

The most important step in solving the ***digital divide*** is to capitalize on thing you know. Most of us use technology more than we realize. Televisions, VCRs, voicemail, stereos, microwave ovens, and calculators all present opportunities to use technology in our everyday lives. You do not need a sophisticated computer to model an informed, healthy, and productive use of technology. The approach is always the same, whether it is a VCR or a super computer - take time to understand it and make the technology work for you, rather than getting frustrated and giving up. Whether you realize it, or not, parents (adults) are children's first and foremost role model when it comes to using technology. So, show your child how to get help and exercise patience with technology. When approached positively and with the purposes of enhancing what you already value, using technology can be an exciting experience. Approaching technology with a healthy attitude and the willingness to explore can yield enriching results is a must.

Here are a couple of ideas you can do right now:

talk 2 your child about technology

Encourage your child to use computers to enhance what they want to do anyway. If you have a home computer, model this be searching for information together. Whether you are planning a family (or business) trip, cooking a special dinner, or in need of a weather forecast. You are sure to find plenty of information on the Internet. Emphasize to your children that the computer is a tool to help them with their goals; it is not an end in itself. Discuss with your children the ways communication and using computers can enhance research. In addition, discuss the advantages and disadvantages of different technologies with your child. For what purposes is it better to use computers? When is it worth it to save the time, and when is it better to do something without relying on an automated or virtual medium? Tell them about your use of computer at work – things you like and dislike. Your child is living in a world changing at a much greater rate than when you were a child. Talk about the rate of change and the challenges of adapting to new ways of doing things. This can and will open their minds to begin thinking of life of adapting versus staying in the same spot.

make PC's work for you

Research has revealed that demographic characteristics not only determine _whether_ and _where_ one uses the Internet, but _how_ a person uses the Internet. Income, education, race, and gender, among other characteristics, strongly influence what a person does online. They can affect not only the types of Internet activities and searches, but also the nature of a person's e-mail. This is true regarding both Internet use at home and Internet use outside the home. More significantly, people are using the Internet to improve and advance their current status. For example, those who are unemployed are using the Internet to find jobs, and those with lower incomes and many minorities are using the Internet to take courses or do school research. The data, therefore, shows the Internet is becoming not only a source of information, communication, and entertainment, but also a tool that can help users help themselves.

Digital Divide: An Equation needing a Solution

use PC's at home to. . .

- *Email*
- *Information search*
- *Check News*
- *Take courses*
- *Do work related tasks*
- *Shop, pay bills*
- *Job search*
- *Entertainment / Games*

As the following illustrations states, more people that use a computer at home accesses email at home compared to playing games.

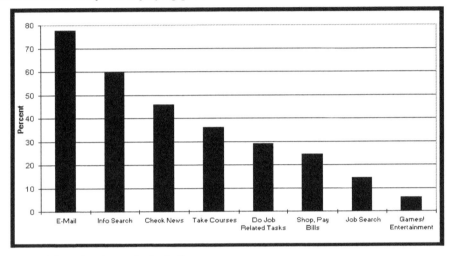

take advantage of what's free

Many art and science museums have computers available to visitors, and most public libraries have Internet access as well. Take your child to the library and use the Internet to find some information of interest to both of you until you can obtain your own. Model curiosity and skill building by asking the librarian to help you use the Internet. Remember, it is your comfort and learning habits that will have a lasting effect on your child.

Overall, as I attempted to illustrate, you need to do whatever you can to help the children around you--including nieces, nephews, grandchildren, as well as your own youngsters-- to understand and appreciate the value of technology.

Type of occupations (employment)

There are *thousands* of computer-related jobs available today. And many more are being created almost everyday. Here is a short list of occupations:

NOTE: *asterisk represents that this occupation is very demanding in the industry as of 2006.

- *3D Animation / Graphic Design*
- *Architecture*
- *Business information systems*
- **Computer forensics*
- **Consulting / Project Manager*
- **Contingency Planning / Disaster Recovery*
- *Data processing / Data Entry*
- *Engineering*
- *Mainframe Systems Support*
- **Networks: Local Area Networks (LANs), Wide Area Networks (WANs)*
- **Programming systems development / Analysis / Database Development and Administration*
- **Quality Assurance (QA) / System Analyst / Technical Auditor / Tester*
- *Sales*
- **Security*
- **Support Services (Security, Policy, Help Desk, Training. etc.)*
- *Technical Writing*
- **Telecommunications (VOIP)*
- *Training*
- *Web Design / Support / e-Commerce*

http://jobsearchtech.about.com/od/computerjob13

http://monster.com

Case Study – Small Business Entrepreneur

Sam is a techno-hands-on kind of guy who's a local entrepreneur. His day starts at 5:30 am when he gets up, freshens up, walks the dog, and while walking his dog, checks his email via his handheld device. Comes back home, feeds the dog, grabs a cup of coffee, kisses his wife and two children good-bye, then off to the office. He arrives at approximately 7:30 am, where he prepares to meet with for a client meeting. The rest of the day is a blur of calls, putting out fires and additional ad hoc meetings: his banker, his accountant, his suppliers, etc... He usually leaves his office around 5:30 pm with a briefcase full of reports to read for upcoming projects. Sometimes he will head straight home to his wife and two children, but often times he heads to the gym if he doesn't have dinner with a client.

Sam may sound like you, or many hardworking small-business owners you know. But there's one important difference: *he is always connected to his clients and their information.*

Like other consultants around the country, Sam needs access to information at any point of the day regardless of his location, what time it is, and what is going on around him. So, he did what many consultants have to do in order to stay competitive: *he invested in technology.* Not only to stay current, but more importantly to stay competitive.

In 2005, U.S. entrepreneurs spent $125 billion on information technology and telecommunications, up from $120 billion in 2004, according to a confidential AMI-Partners study that Microsoft agreed to share with *FSB*. And a recent HP survey found that most small-business owners (81%) plan to increase technology spending by 20% over the next two to three years.

http://ami-usa.com

The small-business technology market isn't just big - it's also extremely profitable. Yet the sector is still underserved from a technology perspective. Although 93% of all small businesses use PCs, only 42% of those companies are equipped with a local area network, according to AMI-Partners. Only a third of them (33%) use laptop PCs, although that percentage is expected to rise as laptop prices fall.

CONCLUSION: Sam could also be a lady (short for Samantha). Regardless of gender, Sam is not alone. This character is part of a veritable menagerie industry that is beginning to flourish and shape technology in it's own special way.

Too often techno-savvy people are accused of being arrogant and isolation from the world. With this comes the stereotypes of engineers, who are brilliant geeks with limited social skills and inadequate personal hygiene, who grew up pounding out code in their bedrooms, dreaming of how to hack the world's national computer bank and relating to actual human beings only through the role-playing video games.

In fact, this stereotype has long-been put to bed. Most computer consultants are no different than other industry consultants: *they both have a strong education in science and/or business administration and also posses a certain "on your feet" thinking skills.*

Digital Divide: An Equation needing a Solution

Computer consultants provides a certain level of expert advice with recommendations to a department/agency as the basis for making a decision or taking a certain course of action to resolve something or enhance a function *including:*

- *providing expert advice on technical and professional matters;*
- *carrying out research projects, attitudinal surveys, feasibility studies and fact finding investigations where recommendations are made;*
- *developing and designing a benchmarking framework/process and standards; and*
- *providing advice in the development of policy and strategic planning issues.*

In addition, consultants like Sam

- *have High Personal Standards and Expectations*
- *are Obsessive*
- *have a real work ethic*
- *get Real-World Experience*
- *are Creative*
- *possess Courage*

A career in consulting is varied and stimulating because each project presents a new challenge and will give you exposure to new clients, business issues, technologies and people. Many engagements draw on the whole range of our skills and services, and our consulting professionals are expected to lead and manage the many different skills and people in our various workforces. We need people who are able to challenge conventional thought, offer unique perspectives and conceive more innovative solutions for our clients.

In the real world, most entrepreneurs are not tech-savvy people, but people who understand business, and how to match the people who know, with the people who are not informed. The same exist for IT consulting today.

<u>CONCLUSION</u>

Wisdom is knowing what to do next,

skill is knowing how to do it, and

virtue is doing it.

In retrospect, we have seen a society shift from an Industrial Age to an Information Age to now a Digital Age. This reality merits a thoughtful response by policymakers consistent with the needs of Americans in the Information Age.

As the Internet becomes a more mature and pervasive technology, the ***digital divide*** among households of different races, incomes, and education levels may narrow. From that, race matters less at the highest income levels and the gap is narrowing among households of higher income and education levels. Even so, it is reasonable to expect that many people are going to lag behind in absolute numbers for a long time. Education and income appear to be among the leading elements driving the ***digital divide*** today.

In short, we are becoming *two* Americas: *one rich, one poor.* We will pay a steep price if nothing is done to address this crisis. The political obstacles are formidable, but the stakes are too high not to take action in the best interests of our children.

We must challenge the technology industry and our educators to continue to create programs and technology that reach not only this demographic, but also people equally, as well as improve our day-to-day lifestyle.

Let's make one thing crystal clear; in no way am I saying that there isn't a minority presence within the technology industry. I'm proof that there are a number of us that have made it through the rough waters. What I have tried to illustrate in this text is collectively, our demographic doesn't have the same access to the same resources as others – even today.

The following *five* strategies will enable our society to survive and thrive in the new millennium and ready ourselves for the next technological age:

- *Understand and embrace new technology*
- *Be an active participant in the information age*
- *Prepare the next generation of black digerati*
- *Join online communities*
- *Obtain an understanding how e-commerce works*

UNDERSTAND AND EMBRACE NEW TECHNOLOGY

As the world continues to evolve, it has become increasingly difficult to keep up with new technological developments and to understand their implications. Already futurists are talking about an electronic wallet--a smart card that replaces your money, keys, driver's license, medical records, and other necessities. Just around the corner are smart homes that will make the typical family resembling the Jetson's and not the Jefferson's. In addition, are you looking for a new job, or do you want to buy a new home? What about a new car? There are more listings posted on the Web than there are ads in newspapers nowadays. Being online also has its financial benefits. You can pay your bills and keep tabs on your 401(k) plan, plus online trading can be cheaper than using a stockbroker. Some of the lowest prices for goods, especially hard-to-find items, are found at stores whose addresses end with DOT something.

You will be able to capitalize on the forces and trends shaping the world of tomorrow, but only if you are inspired to have the right information and technological tools today. The real hook up is being online. Not only does it enable small businesses to compete with large companies, but also preferential treatment is given to companies that do business with each other electronically.

It seems there's nothing a computer chip can't do once you slip it into the right place. The promise of tomorrow is that you can access any information--from anywhere at anytime within the blink of an eye as long as you are connected.

BE AN ACTIVE PARTICIPANT IN THE INFORMATION AGE.

Beyond the role of public and private partnerships, everyone has a part to play. Overcoming the *digital divide* begins at home. It has become commonplace to have a television set not only in the family room, but in every room. Ideally, families should have more than one computer--one for mom, one for dad (or one for the parents), and another for the kids (shared or individual).

On the other hand, if families continue not to be plugged in, they won't be able to play in the technology game of life. And if you don't play, you can't expect to win.

One way you can help ensure that everyone has access to information technology is by getting your employer to donate computers to schools, or churches, or even families in

Digital Divide: An Equation needing a Solution

the area. Volunteer your services teaching computer and Internet skills at any of the more than 350 Community Technology Centers nationwide.

Visit the CTC Network Website (http://www.ctcnet.org)
The Digital Divide Network (http://www.digital-dividenetwork.org/)
Black Data Processing Association (http://www.bdpa.org/) local chapter
for an extensive listings of volunteer opportunities.

PREPARE THE NEXT GENERATION OF BLACK DIGERATI.

Many opportunities exist in the high-tech sector. Yet, the nation's top tech companies resemble the rest of corporate America. Minorities are moving laterally while other groups are moving up. Also, too few African American students are earning science and engineering degrees. Statistics from National Action Council for Minorities in Engineering (NACME) - *"Math is Power"* campaign show that African American students lose interest in math and science after the sixth grade. Ironically, *Generation Y* has grown up on technology. Today's youth are familiar with interactive characters and 3D graphic video games. Never mind listening to CDs on a Sony Discman – they listen to MP3 players; we're talking about downloading music from the Internet and listening to it on portable digital players and not being subjected to buying full CD's anymore. Don't forget to constantly upgrade your own skills so you can compete in an increasingly technological workforce. Using current technology to educate the next generation must be a priority.

JOIN ONLINE COMMUNITIES.

The World Wide Web has become a powerful medium for bringing about a greater sense of community online and off. The Net has become a meeting place for people to share resources and exchange ideas.

Make no mistake about it, the Internet does has a soulful side to it offering plenty of opportunities for you to network, shop, find jobs, listen to music, view movie trailers, and meet that perfect mate. There are more than a dozen Black-oriented Web portals and destination sites, from NetNoir (netnoir.com), one of the first cyberspace explorers, to BlackPlanet.com, one of the fastest growing community sites today, to HappilySingle.com, a new place for adult singles to meet and interact.

portals

At one side, in particular, Africana.com, is bridging the gap between a national and an international community. In addition, they want their site to be useful and relevant to people's lives. For example, they ran a series `from job to career,' which provided advice on how to package and present yourself.

There are thousands of online communities geared towards just about every interest of today society. And guess what? If there isn't one you that serves your interest, start your own!

http://BlackPlanet.com
http://HappilySingle.com
http://africana.com

Digital Divide: An Equation needing a Solution

OBTAIN AN UNDERSTANDING HOW E-COMMERCE WORKS.

For would-be Internet moguls, private-equity markets are more pliable than ever before. The amount of venture capital investments ballooned to $21 billion in 2000 and over $42 billion in 2004, with Internet companies getting the biggest share. E-commerce is a term referred to conducting business over the Internet, such as buying or paying for something online. This isn't new - what it is an improved way we conduct commerce transactions and has become unavoidable.

e-commerce

All of the major companies have begun bypassing traditional links in the supply chain and shipping direct to buyers. At Amazon.com® (http://amazon.com), you can review a book, compare subjects and once you find the item you want, then make an educated purchase while in the comfort of your own house; or you can purchase airline tickets, at the price you want, select your seat, and print out your boarding pass.

E-commerce has changed the way we all conduct normal transactions. This segment allows individuals, as well as companies the ability to fulfill purchasing needs quickly and without hassle 24 hours a day / 7 days a week.

In addition, the Internet helps us find necessary information to help make an educated decision on a given purchase. With this enhancement of commerce, companies have recognized that so many people, so many businesses, within reach at such low cost, as well as so much potential revenue available to businesses only. This is why e-commerce has become a necessity for businesses today.

Quick facts on e-commerce (at the time of this writing):

- *over 15 million servers on the internet*
- *65 million individual users*
- *over 200,000 domain names issued to businesses in 2004, representing 51% of all domain names issued*
- *the number of web pages doubles every 43 days, and stands over three million in 2004*
- *71% of Canadian small businesses are currently using the internet*
- *44% of Canadian small business owners currently conduct financial transactions online, and another 41% plan to do so*
- *92% of international executives believe the internet will reshape the global marketplace*
- *value of electronic commerce transactions in 1996 was $12 million*
- *value of electronic commerce transactions in 2000 predicted to be $2 billion*
- *value of electronic commerce transactions in 2004 predicted to be $18 billion*
- *estimated amount of business- to-business (B2B) web purchases in 2004 is 80% of $220 billion*
- *B2B e-commerce is expected to grow at a rate of 41%*

NOTE: All money mention above is based on United States.

I would like to believe I have demonstrated that using technology will mean more access to resources never seen before. Your personal lack of technology know-how is not an excuse in order to prevent you from getting involved. We must make technology a priority. Let's make no mistake about it, technology isn't going to replace traditional educational and business concepts - it will continue to enhance many industries. In short, no businesses and individuals can afford to ignore this tremendous development.

Digital Divide: An Equation needing a Solution

Now I've talked about the *digital divide* now for over a hundred pages. In closing, the one thing I must stress is we must take a closer look at ourselves and get involved - keep educating our teachers and mentoring our youth. At the end of the day, it's still people who inspire each other, not the tools they use. It is paramount for minorities to harness all the information the internet has to offer from every possible venue.

There are no signs that the digital economy will slow down. It will continue to spur job growth and open the doors to prosperity for Web-savvy entrepreneurs and small business owners. In the 21st century, minorities must make sure that they, too, share in the spoils of the digital revolution.

I guess it's safe to say, no. . . . the *digital divide* is not based on hype or propaganda.

Develop a passion for learning.

If you do, you will never cease to grow. ~ Anthony J. D'Angelo

Glossary

Nothing in education is so astonishing as the amount of ignorance it accumulates in the form of facts. ~ Henry Adams

When talking with students, computer coordinators, or anyone technical, we often confront a language barrier. The use of terms that isn't fully understood, especially acronyms, may make things seem very confusing. I have provided a list of buzz words, acronyms, important organizations, popular web site, etc…, to assist in understanding the techno-mumbo-jumbo used today (in alphabetical order). I hope you find the listing very helpful.

@: - *Pronounced at sign or simply as at, this symbol is used in e-mail addressing to separate the user's name from the user's domain name, both of which are necessary in order to transmit e-mails. For example, the e-mail address digitaldivide@sefitch.com indicates that the user named digitaldivide receives e-mail "at," (or @) the sefitch.com domain.*

AAC: *Advanced Audio Codec. A new technology for compressing music files that's used in the Apple iPod and iTunes. Many say it will replace MP3. See http://www.vialicensing.com/products/mpeg4aac/standard.html*

Access point: *An access point is a piece of equipment that sends and receives wireless signals to and from a Wi-Fi-enabled PC, wirelessly connecting it to a network or the Internet. An access point transmits a Wi-Fi signal that multiple users can share simultaneously.*

Anti-Virus: *An application designed to search for viruses and repair files on a computer.*

Application: *Program or software. Programs that allow to you accomplish certain tasks such as write letters, analyze numbers, sort files, manage finances, draw pictures, and play games.*

Arrow Keys: *The keys on computer keyboard used to move the cursor up, down, left, or right on your screen.*

AUP (Acceptable Use Policy): *A set of rules and guidelines that are set up to regulate Internet use and to protect the user.*

Backspace / Delete key: *Key on a keyboard that moves the cursor to the left one space at a time*

Back-Up: *A second, safe copy of a file, program or any kind of data. All-important data on your computer should be backed up and kept in a safe location in the case of hard disk failure or computer theft.*

BBEdit: *A program used by HTML programmers to create Web pages. The rest of us use WYSIWYG programs such as Dream weaver.*

BBBOnline: *mission is to promote trust and confidence on the Internet through the BBBOnLine Reliability and Privacy Seal Programs. BBBOnLine's web site seal programs allow companies with web sites to display the seals once they have been evaluated and confirmed to meet the program requirements.*

BlackPlanet.com, *one of the fastest growing community sites today.*

Blog: *is short for weblog. A weblog is a journal (or newsletter) that is frequently updated and intended for general public consumption. Blogs generally represent the personality of the author or the Web site. A blog is basically a journal that is available on the web. The activity of updating a blog is "blogging" and someone who keeps a blog is a "blogger." Blogs are typically updated daily using software that allows people with little or no technical background to update and maintain the blog. An online journal.*

Bold: *A style of text that makes a letter or word darker and thicker to stand out in a document.*

Booting: *The process of loading the operating system software into memory to start up a computer. Also called starting.*

Buttons: *A hot spot used in multimedia applications to navigate from one place to another or to activate elements (e.g., sound, movies, animation).*

Button Bar: *A little box on your screen that you click on with your mouse to accomplish a task. Most buttons contain small pictures (icons) that display what they do, such as a small printer that can be clicked on to print a document. It's also recognized as a horizontal strip of buttons near the top of a window. It provides shortcuts for commonly used commands. Some programs let you choose to hide or display the button bar, and mix and match buttons to customize a button bar. Also known as a toolbar.*

Byte, Kilobyte, Megabyte, Gigabyte: *A **byte** is a unit of computer memory. It is a very small unit. Just to give you an idea about how small it is, the computer needs one byte of memory to remember or store one character! That is why computer file sizes are usually expressed in **Kilobytes** (roughly 1000* bytes) and your computer's*

*RAM (Random Access Memory) is usually expressed in **Megabytes** (roughly 1000* kilobytes), and your hard drive is usually measured in **Gigabytes** (roughly 1000 megabytes). To simplify matters, remember this:*

- *1000 Bytes = 1 Kilobyte (KB)*
- *1000 Kilobytes = 1 Megabyte (MB)*
- 1000 Megabytes = 1 Gigabyte (GB)
- *One Kilobyte is actually 1024 bytes

All new computers sold today come with a minimum of 128 megabytes of RAM and most have 256 megabytes installed.

Cable modem: *can transfer data at 500 kbps or higher, compared with 28.8 kbps for common telephone line modems, but the actual transfer rates may be lower depending on the number of other simultaneous users on the same cable. A faster, affordable bandwidth solution of access the Internet at home and/or at a small business.*

Caps Lock key: *Key on a keyboard that is used to key all capital letters.*

CD-ROM: *Stands for Compact Disk Read Only Memory. It's an optical disk that can only be read from and not written to.*

Cell: *The space at the intersection of a row and column in a spreadsheet.*

Central City: *A central city is the largest city within a "metropolitan" area, as defined by the Census Bureau. Additional cities within the metropolitan area can also be classified as "central cities" if they meet certain employment, population, and employment/residence ratio requirements.*

Chart: *A way to present information from a spreadsheet in the form of graphs or tables.*

Circle Graph: *A picture showing the relationship of two or more sets of data using a circler.*

Clip Art: *A series of picture files that are stored on a disk that can be "clipped" and pasted into a document.*

Column: *The vertical divisions of a spreadsheet that intersect that horizontal division (rows) to form cells in which data can be entered.*

Common operating environment (or COE): *A business with a network environment, where a number of employees have access to a central data depository that will establish document naming conventions, determine the file structure, grant access as appropriate, and safeguard information.*

Community Access Center: *A public place where a local community can use computers, the Internet, or other new technologies. Community access centers can include libraries, schools, community centers, and other public access points. Communities may vary as to which public access points serve as community access centers.*

Computer: *A "computer" is defined for Current Population Surveys as a personal or home workstation having a typewriter-like keyboard connected to a laptop computer, mini-computer, or mainframe computer.*

Copy: *To highlight a section or whole document and leave it unaffected but make a duplicate and put it another place.*

CNet™ (http://www.cnet.com) *reviews many products and rates them. Go to CNet.com and search "security," "virus protection," "spyware protection," or "firewall." You can order the list by review date or highest rated.*

CPU (Central Processing Unit): *The main component, or "brain," that allows computers to do millions of calculations per second and makes it possible for users to write letters and balance your checkbook.*

Cursor: *This is where the action is located on your screen, represented by a flashing line. When you type on your keyboard, the information appears at the cursor.*

Cyber-Crime ('computer crime') *is any illegal behavior directed by means of electronic operations that targets the security of computer systems and the data processed by them. In a wider sense, 'computer - related crime' can be any illegal behavior committed by means of, or in relation to, a computer system or network, however, this is not cyber-crime*

Data: *A general term for pieces of information that a computer processes.*

Database: *A collection of data organized for search and retrieval.*

Delete: *A key used to erase characters.*

Desktop: *The background on the windows, menus, and dialog boxes on a PC. It is supposed to represent a desk.*

Desktop publishing: *Using features of word processing/DTP software to format and produce documents, letters, reports, flyers, and newsletters with graphics.*

DHTML: *Dynamic HTML. Language used to program Web pages that change based on what the user does, using style sheets and scripts. Not for the faint of heart.*

Disk drive: *The device that reads from and writes to a floppy disk or hard disk.*

Diskette: *The most common storage device used with microcomputers. 1. (also floppy disk) A flexible disk, made of thin plastic and magnetically coated. A jacket that has openings to allow the disk drive to read or write*

Digital Divide: An Equation needing a Solution

information protects it. 2. (also rigid disk) A floppy disk covered by a hard plastic jacket with a metal slide moved to read or write information.

Driver: *A driver is the software needed to run a hardware device, such as a printer, sound card, monitor, or scanner. New computers usually come with all the drivers already installed. But if you buy a new printer later or upgrade you video card, you will have to install the driver for it from the manufacturer. The driver may be stored on a floppy disk, a CD Rom, or you may have to download it from the manufacturer's web site. Usually the driver comes packaged with the software that came with your new hardware. You just have to install it.*

Domain: *The part of an Internet address that identifies where a person's account is located. For example, in the address* mailto:info@sefitch.com *the domain is everything after the @.*

Download: *transferring information electronically from another computer to your computer.*

DSL: *(Digital Subscriber Loop) a family of digital telecommunications protocols designed to allow high speed data communication over the existing copper telephone lines between end-users and telephone companies. When two conventional modems are connected through the telephone system (PSTN), it treats the communication the same as voice conversations*

Edit: *To make changes in a document or presentation.*

E-mail: *The digital transmission of a message from one person to another using a communications network.*

Enter / Return: *The key used to begin a new line in a word processor, or to enter information into a spreadsheet. It is the same as clicking OK in a dialog box.*

.EXE: *Executable. Filename extension used for application programs in the Windows operating system. Many viruses often arrive unwanted with this moniker. Never open an .exe file whose provenance you doubt.*

Federal Communication Commission: *(FCC) is an independent United States government agency, directly responsible to Congress. The FCC was established by the Communications Act of 1934 and is charged with regulating interstate and international communications by radio, television, wire, satellite and cable. The FCC's jurisdiction covers the 50 states, the District of Columbia, and U.S. possessions.*

File: *A set of related records in a database.*

File Sharing: *Sharing files, usually MP3 music, videos or software, over a network of computer. Programs such as Kazaa, Kazaa light and Grokster enable you to download and upload files on a network of millions of computers around the world. See Links Page.*

Firewall: *Technology that prevents users from visiting inappropriate web sites, and protects the network from unauthorized users.*

Font: *A specific design for a set of letters and characters.*

Format or Re-format: *Disk formatting is the process of preparing a hard disk drive or other storage medium for use by the operating system. Formatting essentially creates the file system structure that the operating system requires for data to be stored on the drive.*

There are several different file systems, such as FAT, Fat32, and NTFS.

Formatting a disk destroys all data that is on it, including Windows Operating System. For this reason, before any disk is formatted, backups of important data should be made. A backup of all device drivers should also be made. The advantage of re-formatting is that a computer running on a severely corrupted operating system can be reverted to a fresh and new state. Formatting a disk also eliminates all accumulated digital garbage that has built up over the months or years.

Disks can be formatted with two or more file systems, divided into sections: this is known as partitioning.

Freeware: *Software written and then donated to the public, so anyone is free to copy it and share it with their friends. This is not the same as shareware or commercial software, which is supposed to be paid for.*

FTP (File Transfer Protocol*): A system for transferring files over the Internet, used most often to move files between your computer and a server.*

Gif *(Graphic Interchange Format -*Pronounced "jiff."): *A file format for pictures, photographs, and drawings that are compressed so that they can be sent across telephone lines quickly. Format widely used on electronic bulletin boards and the Internet and is limited to 256 colors, so they cannot be used for high-end desktop publishing.*

Graph: *A picture shows the relationship of one or more sets of numbers to each other. Some graph types are line, bar, area, and pie graphs.*

Graphic: *Images/pictures created, edited, and/or published using a computer.*

Hacker: *Computer users who enjoy tinkering with computers as a way to develop new features or who intentionally access a single computer, system or a network without permission to do so.*

Hard Drive: *The hard drive is the main storage device in the computer. It consists of several round platters that spin at either 5400, 7200 or even 10,000 RPM. They range in size from ten or twenty gigabytes right up to 200 gigabytes in a higher end computer.*

Hardware: *The physical equipment of a computer, such as a CPU, storage devices, keyboard, screen, mouse, joystick, printer, speakers, etc.*

Highlight or Select: *To choose part of a document by clicking and dragging over it with the mouse to highlight the text.*

Home Page: *An introductory screen on a web page on the World Wide Web, used to welcome visitors. A home page can include special text or graphics on which you click to jump to related information on other pages on the Web.*

Home Row: *Keys on the keyboard with fingers of the left hand are on A-S-D-F and fingers on the right hand on J-K-L-;*

Host: *The name given to a computer directly connected to the Internet. Host computers are associated with computer networks, online services, or bulletin board systems.*

Hot spot: *A hot spot is a place where a service provider offers users Wi-Fi Internet access in a given location.*

HTML: *Hyper Text Markup Language. Coding used in web pages. Geeks write it directly; the rest of us use web-page editors that write the HTML for us.*

Hyperlink or Hypertext (HTTP): *Special text when clicked jumps the user from one related topic to another.*

HTTPS: *a unique protocol that is simply providing a secure path to a web site. See **SSL** for further details.*

Install: *The steps taken to copy files of an un-installed program on to your computer's operating system and then configuring it with the options that you require.*

Intellectual property: *Ideas put into actions, such as writing, music, art, computer code, and inventions that can be protected under copyright or patent laws.*

Information Highway: *A term used when discussing information networks of the future, which will likely carry video and audio as well as computer data.*

IP (Internet Protocol): *Without it there'd be no Internet, no World Wide Web. It's the standard syntax used to assemble and manage the packets of data that send information back and forth across the net.*

Input: *The process of entering information into a computer.*

Internet: *A worldwide system of interconnected networks allowing for data transmission between millions of computers. The Internet is usually accessed using Internet Service Providers.*

Internet Service Provider (ISP): *An organization or company that provides Internet access to individuals or organizations.*

Jpeg *(Joint Photographic Experts Group):* *A standard for shrinking graphics so they can be sent faster between modems and take up less space on your hard drive. These graphics can be reduced to 5 percent of their original size, but the image quality deteriorates. However, compressing graphics to 30 or 40 percent of their original size results in minimal loss of quality. A digital camera uses JPEG compression.*

K (Kilo): *Greek for thousand. A kilobit is a thousand bits of data. A Kilobyte is a thousand bytes, bytes consisting of eight to ten bits, depending on who's counting.*

Keyboard: *An input device resembling a typewriter and consisting of a standardized layout of buttons or keys with symbols, such as letters or numbers that can be entered into a computer by pressing on the keys.*

Keyword: *A word or reference point used to describe content on a web page that search engines use to properly index the page.*

Label: *The term given to the words entered on a spreadsheet usually naming a column.*

LAN: *Local Area Network. The network that connects the computers together in your office or school or maybe even at home. Can be wireless or cabled, most commonly using Ethernet.*

Landscape: *The page setup that permits a document to be printed in a horizontal position.*

Laptop: *A portable personal computer of a size suitable to carry in a small briefcase (portfolio) and rest comfortably on one's legs.*

Line graph: *A graph used to display trends and compare data.*

Line spacing: *The span between lines of text.*

Linear: *Moving in a straight line or path; a multimedia presentation that moves in a straight line from image to image.*

Links: *Connections that bridge one image, page, or word to another by clicking on a highlighted word or phrase.*

Log On: *The act of connecting with a computer system and entering your user identification and password.*

Log Off: *The act of signing off of and disconnecting from a computer system.*

Megahertz and Gigahertz: *This is the speed of the computer. One megahertz is one million operations per second. In 1993, my first computer was 33 megahertz, which was considered very fast at that time. Today I have*

Digital Divide: An Equation needing a Solution

a 2300-megahertz or 2.3 gigahertz. These days, computers are running at speeds of up to 2.8 Gigahertz. One Gigahertz is 1000 megahertz so a 2.8 Gigahertz computer is capable of performing 2.8 billion operations per second.

Modem: *A modem is defined as a device used to connect the computer to a telephone line, often for the purpose of connecting to on-line services. A modem can either be located internally in the PC, or can be an external device.*

Monitor: *The device with a screen used to show computer images.*

Motherboard: *These are the devices that are usually on the outside of the computer box or case. They include the keyboard, the printer, the mouse, the scanner, the speakers, etc. The main circuit board in the computer. All other parts of the computer are plugged into the motherboard including the CPU (processor) and RAM (memory).*

Mouse: *A tool used to move the cursor and pointer around the screen.*

Multimedia: *To use a combination of text, pictures, sounds, movies, and/ or animation in a presentation.*

MP3: *MPEG audio layer 3. A scheme for compressing music files. MPEG stands for Motion Picture Expert Group, which designed this method originally for use in compressing digital video.*

NAT (Network Address Translating): *Since every computer on the Internet needs its own unique IP address, and there are not enough addresses to go around, NAT is used in many LAN's to allow more computers to be online, by translating the LAN's address through to the individual computers.*

Network: *A system of connected computers that allows the sharing of files and equipment. There are two types of networks: local area network (LAN) and wide area network (WAN).*

Network Interface Card: *often abbreviated as NIC, an expansion board you insert into a computer so the computer can be connected to a network (Local Area Network, private home network, cable modem access, as well as DSL). Most NICs are designed for a particular type of network, protocol, and media.*

Non-Linear: *Not moving in a straight line or path; a multimedia presentation that transitions from one image to another in an order that is preset, but not necessarily in a straight path - Example: a non-linear presentation can transition from image 1 to image 3 and back to image 1. using menus/branching.*

Numeric Keypad: *The portion of a keyboard, set up like an adding machine or calculator used to enter numbers and equations quickly into the computer.*

Online Resources: *Internet information available to a computer user.*

Online Safety: *Precautions taken to protect personal information and images from being misused by others.*

OS X Operating System X (Ten): *The software that performs the basic operations on the new Apple® Macintosh™ computers. based on the Unix™ operating system, OS X and Linux are the leading (and growing and relatively virus-free) competitors to the Windows™ operating system from Microsoft®.*

Operating System: *software, which handles the interface to peripheral hardware, schedules tasks, allocates storage, and presents a default interface to the user when no application program is running.*

Page Set Up: *The term in reference to the way a document is formatted to print.*

Partitioning: *A method of dividing a large hard drive into smaller chunks that can each be assigned a separate drive letter. For instance, an 80 Gigabyte drive might be partitioned into four 20 gigabyte drives, each with its own drive letter; C, D, E and F.*

Password: *A code for the security protection to allow access to a computer or the computer programs.*

Paste: *To insert the last information that was cut or copied into a document. Cut and paste can be used to move information within or between documents.*

PC (Personal Computer): *See Computer for a description.*

PDA (Personal Digital Assistant): *a small, hand-held computer typically providing calendar, contacts and note taking, but may include other applications, such as web access and media player.*

Peripherals: *any part of a computer other than the CPU, or working memory (i.e., disks, keyboards, monitors, mice, printers, scanners, tape drives, speakers, camera, etc...)*

Pictogram: *Pictures used to create a bar graph chart*

Pie Graph: *Circle graph divided into pieces that look like portions of a pie.*

Piracy: *The unauthorized duplication and distribution of copyright-protected software.*

PNG (Portable Network Graphics): *A scheme for compressing image files, most often seen as a filename extension. Though all the new browsers can handle .png files, they are not used as much as .gif and .jpg images.*

Portrait: *The default page setup that prints the document vertically.*

Print: *To put what is on the computer screen on paper. It creates a paper copy of the document created on the computer.*

Printer: *A hardware device used to make a paper copy of what is created on the computer.*

Probeware: *Computer assisted data collection tools*

Public Domain: *Software written and then donated to the public. Anyone can use and copy public domain software free of charge, but it is not always the same quality as commercial software.*

PUBACCESS: *Internet usage at a public library or community center.*

QWERTY: *Not really an acronym, it's what American keyboards are called. French keyboards are called AZERTY. Look on your keyboard and you will see why. But the other widely used method of laying out the keys, Dvorak, puts AOEUI on the middle row.*

RAM (Random Access Memory): *is the little integrated circuit board with a bunch of memory chips on it that plug into your motherboard. RAM allows information to be temporarily stored or accessed by the operating system and any programs being run. When a program operates, it uses a certain amount of the computer's RAM. A computer with 512 Mb of RAM will be able to run many more programs simultaneously than a computer with 128 Mb of RAM. Depending on what you are using your computer for, a good rule of thumb is to install as much RAM as you can afford.*

Record: *A collection of related field and entries.*

Retrieve: *To load a file from a diskette or hard drive with the intent to view, print or observe.*

Row: *The horizontal divisions in a spreadsheet named with a number.*

RTSP (Real Time Streaming Protocol): *A syntax for arranging the data in packets and managing their passage over the Internet, used for video and audio streaming such as QuickTime and Real Video. Since it uses UDP packets, some school firewalls block RTSP streams.*

Save: *To storing information on a floppy disk, hard drive or CD for later use. Work should be saved often, every 5 or 10 minutes, to make sure your latest changes are safely recorded.*

Save As: *To save a document with a new name.*

Scanner: *A scanner is like a camera for your computer. It takes a picture of whatever you place on its glass surface. Once you close the lid and start the scanner program, the scanner takes a picture that shows up on your computer screen, ready to be printed or exported into a image-editing program.*

Search: *To look for specific information on the Internet or computer.*

Search Engine: *Software that searches gathers and identifies information from a database based on keywords, indices, titles and text.*

Search Strategies: *There are 3 basic ways to begin a search.*
1. *Try to guess at the URL.*
2. *Use Subject directories provided by some search engines. Subject, categories, and subcategories that can be used for keyword search or to browse the categories group the selected resources.*
3. *Use a search engine for large searches using unique keywords or combinations of keywords to narrow the search.*

Security: *Protection of computer, computer files or a computer network from use without permission of the owner or owners.*

Select or Highlight: *To choose part of a document by clicking and dragging over it with the mouse to highlight the text.*

Server: *A special computer used to store programs and files, and then sends it out to other computers one or all at a time.*

Service provider: *a company or individual that provides a service (i.e., Internet, technical support, communication)*

Shareware: *Programs like public domains but ones for which the author / developer request a donation if you use the software.*

SMTP (Simple Mail Transfer Protocol): *The system of arranging and tracking packets of data in email messages that travel across the internet. Your emails are sent by, and received by, an SMTP server.*

Software/Application: *Programs that allow you to accomplish certain tasks such as write letters, analyze numbers, sort files, manage finances, draw pictures, and play games.*

Sound Card: *This is one of the little boards the plug-in to the motherboard. It's the part that makes all the sound you hear when you use the computer. This card enables you to play music CDs on your computer. The speaker, the microphone, and joystick all plug into to the sound card. Technically speaking, it is a digital to analog and analog to digital converter.*

Sort: *Arranging information in a specific order (usually ascending and descending).*

Space bar: *Key on a keyboard that spaces the cursor forward one space at a time and produces a blank space when pressed.*

Spreadsheet: *An application that can be used to do calculations, analyze and present data. It includes tools for organizing, managing, sorting and retrieving data and testing "what if " statements. It has a chart feature that displays numerical data as a graph.*

Digital Divide: An Equation needing a Solution

SSID (service Set Identifier): *An SSID is a network setting on your mobile device or notebook (laptop) computer that enables it to identify wireless networks in your area. An SSID consists of a sequence of characters that acts as a network's name.*

SSL *(Secure Sockets Layer): a protocol, designed by Netscape Communications Corporation™, to provide encrypted communications on the Internet.*

Stand Alone Computer: *A computer that does not rely upon any other computer or server to work.*

Storyboard: *A graphic organizer used for planning and developing a multimedia report/presentation. The contents, layout, and formatting of each card/slide and the linking together of the cards/slides.*

Streaming: *A technique for transferring data such that is can be processed as steady and continuous stream of audio and/or video.*

T1 (Telecommunications 1 megabit): *A way of describing the bandwidth of a communications connection. If your school is connected to the Internet with a T1 line, you can pass more data more quickly than a school with a cable modem or ISDN line.*

Table: *Columns and rows of cells that can be filled with text that are used to organize information*

Telecommunication: *The act of sending and receiving information, such as data, text, pictures, voice, and video. The exchange of information can be within a building or around the globe.*

Telecomputing: *The act of sending (or receiving) information to another computer via modem and phone line or local area networks (LAN). The exchange of information can be within a building or around the globe.*

Terra firma: *Solid ground; dry land.*

Thesaurus: *A feature in most word processors used to replace a word in a document with one that is more suitable and adds variety to your writing.*

TRUSTe®: *is an independent, nonprofit enabling trust based on privacy for personal information on the Internet. We certify and monitor web site privacy and email policies, monitor practices, and resolve thousands of consumer privacy problems every year.*

UDP (User-Defined Protocol): *Yet another method for arranging and managing data packets that flow across the Internet, this one open to a variety of syntaxes. UDP packets are often used for streaming audio and video, such as RTSP.*

Upload: *sending a file from your computer to another computer.*

URL Address (Uniform Resource Locator): *Website address. Example: http://www.stevenefitch.com/*

USB: *USB stands for Universal Serial Bus. It is a port through which data passes from the computer to an external device. Printers, mice, scanners, digital cameras, joysticks and many other devices are now connected to the computer via the USB port. A USB device is able to be plugged in and unplugged while the computer is running. This is called hot swapping. Most computer components are available today with the USB with a top data transfer speed of 12 Megabytes per second. There is also a newer version of USB called USB2. This new interface can transfer data at speeds of up to 480 Megabytes per second or 40 times faster than the original USB.*

User name: *First part of an e-mail address. Example: JDoe is the user name of the following e-mail address. JDoe@yahoo.com*

Value: *The term for a number in a spreadsheet that can be added, subtracted, multiplied or divided.*

Vandalism: *The intentional act of destroying computer files or computer networks.*

Video Card: *This card is used to process the video signal that goes to your monitor. The faster the processor speed and the more memory it has, the better. They can usually be identified as a video card by the built in cooling fan.*

Virus: *A computer program designed to damage computer files. A computer program that can reproduce by changing other programs to include a copy of itself.*

VR (Virtual Reality): *Not what a philosopher might think, VR refers to a wide range of technologies that attempt to produce the perception of the real world through representations of digital data. Often used to describe three-dimensional applications such as QuickTime VR.*

Web: *commonly known as World Wide Web. See WWW below.*

Web address: *Universal Resource Locator (URL). Example: http://www.stevenefitch.com/*

Webopedia.com: *an electronic dictionary used on the Internet for FREE.*

WebTV®: *WebTV® is the most widely used system for accessing the Internet through television sets. A WebTV® unit connects to a television set, much like a VCR, and to a telephone line to send and receive data. This data is then displayed on the television, rather than a computer monitor. WebTV® Networks, Inc. is a subsidiary of the Microsoft® Corporation.*

Wi-Fi: *Wi-Fi, is short for wireless fidelity, is the more well known term for high-speed wireless access to your network or the Internet. Wireless-enabled devices, like your notebook (laptop) computer, can detect a Wi-Fi signal – setting you free from cables and phone cords.*

Wikipedia™ *(pronounced wiki-pi-di-a or we-ki) is a multilingual Web-based free-content encyclopedia wiki service. Wikipedia™ is written collaboratively by volunteers, allowing most articles to be changed by anyone with access to a web browser.*

Wireless network card: *Wireless network card is a credit card size accessory that send and receives wireless signals back and forth with an access point, allowing someone to detect a WiFi network and get connected.*

Word processing: *Using keyboarding skills to produce documents such as letters, reports, manuals, and newsletters.*

Word wrap: *This occurs when you get to the end of a line and continue typing the text will then go to the next line.*

Digital Divide: An Equation needing a Solution

Worm: *A computer file designed to do damage that goes through a computer and possibly a network*

WWW (World Wide Web): *The section of the Internet that allows access to text, graphics, sound, and even video. The Web takes you to a specific site (location) on the Internet. A lot of free information can be found on the WWW.*

WYSIWYG: *WYSIWYG is an acronym for "What You See Is What You Get" and is pronounced "wizzy wig." WYSIWYG simply means that the text and graphics shown on your screen exactly match your printout.*

XML (eXtensible Markup Language): *Like HTML, a coding system for designing web pages. In XML, you define your own tags, and can adjust them to display differently depending on the way the data is used.*

Y2K (Year 2 Kilo): *Shorthand to refer to the year 2000, when we all feared our computers would crash because we now needed four instead of two digits to represent the year. You will still find software labeled* Y2K compliant. *Did your computer survive?*

ZIP: *Zipped file, or Zip disk. The first is a filename extension used to denote files that have been compressed using the Zip method. The second is a type of disk storage, commonly called a Zip disk.*

NOTES

NOTES

APPENDIX

Learn not only to find what you like, learn to like what you find. ~ Anthony J. D'Angelo

[i] http://en.wikipedia.org/wiki/Digital_divide

[ii] **Chicago Tribune**, 2/7/01

[iii] **Washington Post**, 6/18/01

[iv] http://www.webenglish.com.tw/encyclopedia/en/wikipedia/d/di/digital_divide.html

[v] http://www.toptags.com/aama/events/jtenth.htm

[vi] http://www.cps.edu

[vii] US Department of Commerce: http://www.doc.gov or http://www.ntia.doc.gov/reports/anol/index.html

[viii] Dr. Tony Jackson - Black Violence: Real Issues and Real Solutions: http://www.gibbsmagazine.com/Tony%20Violence%201.htm

[ix] http://www.ecommercetimes.com/story/3953.html

[x] http://www.markle.org/downloadable_assets/digitaldivide_openresearch.pdf

[xi] http://www.salon.com/june97/21st/cool970605.html

[xii] http://www.playitcybersafe.com/cybercrime/

[xiii] http://en.wikipedia.org/wiki/Gender_gap

[xiv] http://www.law.northwestern.edu/journals/njtip/v2/n1/2
Women accounted for 50.6 percent of U.S. Internet users in December 2000 according to the Pew Internet and American Life Foundation. Janet Kornblum, *Web Users Look Like America, Only Richer*, USA TODAY, Feb. 8, 2002, *at* http://www.usatoday.com/tech/news/2001-02-19-ebrief.htm (last visited Jan. 26, 2004).

[xv] Electronic Bill of Rights, proposed by Frank W. Connolly (American University) http://courses.cs.vt.edu/~cs3604/lib/WorldCodes/Bill_of_Rights.html

[xvi] NetNoir, Inc., (http://www.netnoir.com), a leading multimedia company promoting creating and distributing distinctive Black/African American programming and commercial applications for all forms of interactive media.

[xvii] Dr. Ben Carson (http://www.hopkinschildrens.org/pages/news/carson.html), is director of pediatric neurosurgery at the Johns Hopkins Children's Center, a position he has held since 1984. He holds appointments in the departments of neurosurgery, oncology, plastic surgery, and pediatrics at the Hopkins School of Medicine.